after a fashion

This book is published in association with Aer Lingus and the major RTE television series 'After A Fashion'.

after a fashion

a history of the Irish fashion industry
Robert O'Byrne

TOWN
HOUSE
DUBLIN

With thanks to: David and Tina Heffernan who first suggested the television series whence came this book; the designers, journalists, photographers, models and stylists associated with fashion – Irish and otherwise – who were interviewed, addressed, pestered and harassed for their assistance: Liz Cleary for her helpful material on Neilli Mulcahy; the crew who had to tolerate me while they were filming the television series; Marie Heaney who edited the book: Polly Devlin who first read it and gave me lots of helpful advice: and all those friends who promised to buy the book once it was published (I expect you now to keep your promises).

First published in 2000 by

Town House and Country House Ltd.,
Trinity House, Charleston Rd.,
Ranelagh, Dublin 6.

pbk ISBN: 1-86059-115-9
HBK ISBN: 1-86059-132-9
© Daniel Productions Ltd., 2000

A CIP catalogue record for this book is available from the British Library.

Designed by Wendy Williams Design

Printed in Ireland by ColourBooks Ltd, Baldoyle Industrial Estate, Dublin.

contents

Robert O'Byrne writes for THE IRISH TIMES on style in all its forms, from clothing and fashion to architecture. He also writes reviews for the books section, and appears regularly on RTE radio and television. After a Fashion is his first book, written to coincide with the RTE Television series of the same name, and he is currently writing a biography of Hugh Lane.

Dedicated to M.D.: the most fashionable woman in Ireland

When I started working on this project, aspiring wags (and there were far too many of them) liked to remark that, since my chosen topic was a history of Irish fashion, the result would be a very slim volume. In fact, the story of fashion in Ireland – at least during the second half of the twentieth century – has been as rich as that anywhere else.

I remember being in Sydney for Australian Fashion Week in May 1998, during which a very fine book on the country's fashion was published. Almost none of the names mentioned in it were familiar to me but that was a reflection of my ignorance, not their talents. (I cannot resist pointing out that Australia's most successful contemporary designer both at home and abroad is Collette Dinnigan who, as her name indicates, is of Irish parentage.) It is, therefore, just as likely that the majority of Australians will know little or nothing about Irish fashion.

The industry today may be global but it is also extremely parochial and concentrated in just four centres – London, Paris, New York and Milan – with only the last of these emerging over the past thirty years to challenge the established hegemony of the other three. Ireland cannot hope to match their authority, although I do dearly love those covers of *Harper's Bazaar* and *Vogue* from the 1950s, on which Dublin is ranked as an equal player with London and Paris.

That our capital should have been held in such high esteem among the international fashion press at this period is all the more surprising given the circumstances in Ireland. The fashion industry appeared here with astonishing rapidity and maturity despite, rather than because of, the era's social and economic climate, and thanks primarily to a handful of women who, contrary to the ethos of the age, ran highly successful businesses. Every time I go back over material from the period, I am in awe of the dynamism and verve shown by Sybil Connolly. I do not believe her skills as a designer equalled those of Irene Gilbert, but as a publicist – of herself and of Ireland – she was without equal both then and since. I suspect most people do not realise just how famous she became, or how fast; forty years ago, she was the most renowned Irish woman in the world and her activities were covered not just in the fashion press but even in the social columns of publications such as the *Hollywood Reporter*. Sybil Connolly deserves to be celebrated because she was unique and set a standard which could never be matched.

Although Irish fashion today is more successful overseas than ever before, I suspect it seems to have less support at home than in the past. In the 1990s Ireland's economic expansion, combined with technological changes, has encouraged the country to become global in outlook. One result of this is that Irish fashion can be seen as provincial (frankly, often with justification). It must also compete in a market saturated with international goods. This can be beneficial, since domestic producers will feel obliged to maintain or even raise their standards in the face of competition, but it also leaves them in a vulnerable position.

Designers, like most creative people, like to complain of neglect – often unnecessarily. In this instance, though, I think they have a case to make. The support they require is not financial (appreciated as this might be) but, for want of a better word, emotional. Our designers need to be loved and to know that they are loved. Lainey Keogh articulates this particularly well when she notes that in our shiny new world of cyber-Ireland, there is no place for fashion, no understanding of how it operates, no appreciation of the benefits it can convey. Other countries such as Italy and France cherish their fashion industries because they realise these can not only provide employment, but also bring prestige to the state. Rather as Louis XIV in the second half of the 17th century established institutions such as the Academie Francaise because these reflected well on his authority, so the French and Italian governments today support their indigenous fashion industries for the unquantifiable but nonetheless real benefit they bring in their wake.

Fashion, of course, can be a very silly business. As an aesthete, I adore its creativity; as an ascetic, I abhor its frivolity. But whatever my personal feelings, I recognise that fashion is an industry capable of making an impact out of proportion to its actual size. This is especially true for a small country like Ireland where just a few names can generate substantial publicity. Our film and pop music industries, while equally modest in scale compared to their equivalents elsewhere, have – like our poets, playwrights and novelists before them – achieved international renown. It would take just a little more encouragement for Irish fashion to follow suit.

And yet that encouragement does not seem forthcoming. For much of the time, Ireland adopts an ambiguous attitude towards fashion, happy to embrace it in success but just as eager to remain aloof from failure. And while Ireland may not necessarily give much support to fashion, she expects fashion to show support for her. In November 1998, Paul Costelloe made some remarks in the *Sunday Times* which were regarded as ill-advised; he dared to suggest that Irish women were not among the world's most stylish. While I might not agree with his phraseology, I concur with the sentiment. The Irish are justly celebrated for many fine qualities, but a sense of style has never been among them. Dubliner Eileen Shields, who works in Manhattan for DKNY, told me one of the characteristics she associates with the Irish is a certain want of polish about their appearance. They always look, she said, "slightly dishevelled". Her remark was not meant as a criticism and ought not to be taken as such. Style, Noel Coward once declared, implies great discipline and this has never been a feature of the Irish temperament. The sense of neglect Irish designers may sometimes feel from their local market is therefore understandable.

Much more worrying than any perceived slight is the very real abandonment of Ireland's traditional crafts, which have tended to be admired more overseas than at home. Lainey Keogh argues in the most trenchant manner that we have been so intent on introducing technologically advanced industry to this country that our old familiar methods of production were ignored as they struggled, usually ineffectually, for survival. At Magee's in Donegal I was shown wonderful swatches of tweed, in dazzling shades of pink and green, hand-woven in small quantities for Irene Gilbert during the 1950s, and made into suits and coats for the designer's customers.

Curiously, I suspect it is in the couture clothing of half a century ago that an answer may lie. Irish fashion cannot, after all, hope to compete in the mass market any longer. Rising labour costs have all but wiped out the Irish clothing industry, since the price of a garment manufactured in the Far East is so much lower than that of one made in Ireland. But the Far East does not possess our reputation, or the traditional craft skills on which this is built. It is in the production of exclusive and expensive goods that Ireland can compete, provided we encourage the maintenance of the skills necessary for their creation. Recently in Brown Thomas, a former government minister asked me if it was possible that someone would be willing to pay the price of £500 being asked for a handbag; the fact of it being offered for sale was sufficient response. There *is* a market, in Ireland and elsewhere, for the rare and the beautiful. The pity is that the handbag in question was Italian and not Irish.

Increasingly, because of domestic manufacturing costs and the want of local skills, our designers arrange to have their clothes made overseas, following the example of fashion labels throughout Europe and the United States. But, as their peers elsewhere have proven, it is possible to run a business in one country while production takes place in another. What matters is that the culture in the designer's home is sympathetic to and supportive of fashion. That would not appear to be the case in Ireland and explains why Lainey Keogh should argue in favour of a more nurturing environment for her profession. Because of its absence, she has spoken of leaving Ireland and others could well follow her example. After all, if a designer no longer manufactures locally, presents each new collection in a foreign country and sells predominantly to the export market, why should he or she wish to stay here? Why not, instead, move to a place where fashion is admired and encouraged? Speaking of the 1970s, Terry Keane remarks that fashion at the time was a very fragile flower. In fact, fragility is a constant feature of the business and that is why the request for more encouragement should be heeded. Otherwise, Ireland might well continue to spawn individual fashion designers, but not a fashion industry in which they can flourish.

From the Jack Clarke Country Wear autumn/winter 1959 collection, this raglan shouldered long jacket and matching pencil skirt are made in a bold check Irish tweed. This fabric was internationally fashionable during the 1950s and, together with linen, helped to establish Ireland as a centre for fashion.

the early days: before 1950

In early May 1950, Jammet's restaurant in Dublin hosted a fashion show presented by a woman called Irene Gilbert. She owned a small shop on South Frederick Street, selling hats as well as some clothing from France and England, and she wanted to give her clientele an idea of what was currently in stock. Almost at the last moment, she decided to include a dozen dresses and suits designed by herself – "just for the devilment" she later explained. But these garments, described as "in every way excellent and extremely smart" by an *Irish Times* woman correspondent, turned out to be the most popular with her audience. Irene Gilbert's career as a fashion designer had begun.

That Jammet's show marks the start of an indigenous Irish fashion industry; until then, there had been no designer of real note resident in the country. There were, of course, plenty of Irish dressmakers and clothing manufacturers, but the work these produced could hardly be regarded as high fashion. In an obituary notice in the *Irish Times* after Irene Gilbert's death, the late Anne, Countess of Rosse, reported that when she had first come to live in Ireland after her marriage in 1935, it was commonly accepted "that ladies of fashion had to resort to the salons of Paris and London to be really well dressed, and that Dublin could produce only dull tweedy suits or dowdy dresses for race meetings or home wear." As if to underline this impression of Irish fashion as hopelessly provincial, Lady Rosse admitted that prior to seeing Irene Gilbert's work, she too "had sought the luxury of Paris or London clothes".

Irish fashion before 1950

Reluctance to support the local fashion industry is understandable once it becomes clear just how lacking in individuality or originality Irish clothing design had been before 1950. Until that date, the people of the country really possessed little or no distinctive style of dress. Indigenous fashion had been almost totally obliterated by the upheavals of the 16th and 17th centuries, and even by 1620 the English lawyer Luke Gernon in his *Discourse of Ireland* could write of the local population: "the better sort are apparelled at all points like the English only they retain their mantle." That mantle, or large cloak, was the last part of native Irish dress to survive but before the century was over it too had all but vanished. Thereafter, as a rule, the inhabitants of Ireland dressed no differently from their nearest neighbours across the Irish Sea. Trade restrictions imposed by successive London governments on the Irish cloth and clothing industries did much to stifle any initiative.

Famously, when Thackeray travelled through Ireland in 1842, it was only in the more remote parts of Connemara that he discovered such distinctive items of local dress as red petticoats and heavy-knitted socks. Otherwise, stylistic differences between the appearance of the Irish and the English were negligible. And while the interwoven strands of the nationalist and arts and crafts movements in the late 19th/early 20th centuries attempted to recreate what was believed to have been native Irish dress, these efforts met with little support and a great deal of derision from the majority of the people. "In the past, it has been quite hard to pin down what Irish style might be," confirms Paula Reed, Style Director of *Condé Nast Traveller*. "There's a physical look that people talk about – that lovely pale complexion and Celtic colouring, red or black hair and a physical delicacy we might have – but that doesn't have much to do with clothes."

There are many reasons why Ireland had been so slow to develop its own fashion industry. "Before 1950," says Elizabeth McCrum of the Ulster Museum, "there weren't the opportunities, either governmental or economic, that came later. Nor were there the expectations that you could work within your own country." Fashion is a luxury and Ireland has not always been able to afford luxuries. Until relatively recently, most of the population had little spare money, certainly not enough for indulgences such as seasonal changes of clothing. And that population has always been quite small, or at least not big enough to sustain many clothing businesses. From Irene Gilbert onwards, successful Irish designers have had to look to overseas markets if they are to survive at home. The domestic clientele has never been sufficient on its own. Furthermore, the thorny question of Irish visual illiteracy – occasionally disputed but nonetheless real - may also have played a part in delaying the development of the country's fashion industry, aided by another much-commented upon feature of the Irish character: an innate conservatism which would not respond well to the radical shifts in style and taste that fashion frequently requires.

Dominance of London

But there is one especially important explanation for Ireland's late entry into fashion – the lure of London. Until Ireland achieved independence, and even for quite some time thereafter, it was to the English capital, rather than Dublin, that the country's most creative talents in a wide variety of areas were drawn. London remains the principal city in Great Britain, explaining why neither Scotland nor Wales have fashion industries of any great substance or repute. Designers like Laura Ashley and Bill Gibb in the past, and Dai Rees and Julian Macdonald today, have never been able to resist moving to London, the centre of British fashion. As headquarters of a large nation's media (as well as the location for a great number of important retailers), the English city's prestige has always overwhelmed that of Dublin, which is both smaller and geographically more on the margins of Europe. This is why even the most established and confident among Irish designers continue to show their collections to the public during London Fashion Week and are happy to be nominated for British fashion awards. "I don't think the sense of having to measure up to another city is particular to us," says Paula Reed. "Having talked to some of the Belgian designers now in Antwerp, I know they have terrible hang-ups about whether or not they size up to Paris or Milan. But maybe because of our history, being in London's shadow has more connotations."

The clothing industry, especially in its upper echelons, has always been urban in character and liable to base itself in the largest and most economically successful cities. Although there are occasional exceptions – Vonnie Reynolds in Bunratty during the 1980s springs to mind – designers understandably gravitate towards where they expect to find most business. It is surely no accident that fashion began in Ireland only when the country's cities, especially Dublin, started to experience rapid growth. Before the second half of the 20th century, London's economic authority was so great that Irish fashion was entirely subsumed by it and any individual identity lost as a result. Until the advent of Irene Gilbert, Irish designers customarily – and understandably – began their careers in London and aspired to become part of the British fashion establishment.

Edward Molyneux

Edward Molyneux, the man usually credited with being Ireland's first great fashion talent, chose to base himself not in London but in Paris. Although his parents were both Irish, he was born in England and began his fashion career there early in the 20th century working for the London house of Lucille. After the First World War (in which he lost the sight of one eye and became a British army captain), Molyneux opened his own atelier on Paris's Rue Royale. This remained his headquarters until he closed the business more than thirty years later. There was, frankly, nothing in his work which could be described as Irish or owing a debt to Ireland. In 1930, famously, he designed the backless white satin evening dress that his loyal client, the actress Gertrude Lawrence, wore when she played Amanda in Noel Coward's "Private Lives". His clothes possessed a streamlined elegance that was international in character, not tied to any one place, like so many of his restless cosmopolitan customers during the inter-war years. Molyneux and his work might well be compared to Eileen Gray, the Wexford-born modernist architect and designer who, like him, spent almost all her professional life in France, never looking back to Ireland.

Digby Morton

This abandonment of their country of origin was repeated by a number of other noteworthy Irish fashion designers working during the first half of the 20th century. Digby Morton was born in 1906 in Dublin, where he studied art and architecture at the Metropolitan School of Art. He then moved to London, first working as a designer at the house of Lachasse (where he was later succeeded by Hardy Amies) before opening his own couture business in 1934. The following year, he was a founder member of the Fashion Group of Great Britain, renamed, during the Second World War, as the Incorporated Society of London Fashion Designers. Morton was always renowned for his smart suiting, an example of which can be seen in Cecil Beaton's most famous wartime fashion photograph; taken in 1941, the picture shows a Morton-clad model standing in the ruins of a bombed London church. Although he did sometimes use Irish fabrics, particularly tweeds, Digby Morton spent all his working life in Britain, where he died in 1983, a decade after his retirement.

John Cavanagh

In many respects, Digby Morton's career found echoes in that of John Cavanagh. Although born in Ireland in 1914, by the age of eighteen Cavanagh was already working for Edward Molyneux in London and studying drawing at college. Later, he moved to work with the older couturier in Paris and, after the Second World War, acted as assistant to Pierre Balmain for four years, until 1951. A year later he opened his own fashion house on Curzon Street in London, where his commissions included the Duchess of Kent's wedding dress in 1961. He shut the business in 1974 but remained in England. Cavanagh's style, like that of Molyneux, was more indebted to Britain than Ireland. He once said, "A couturier worth his name must design in the world-stream of design change," arguing that the clothes produced "should look equally good in London, Paris or New York".

Michael Donnellan

Last among the precursors of indigenous Irish fashion was the designer who kept in closest contact with his native country, Michael Donnellan, later known as Michael of Carlos Place after his premises in London. Born in Ballinlough, County Roscommon in 1915, he originally studied medicine in Dublin before moving to England to attend the British Fashion Institute. Following the example of Digby Morton, he first worked for Lachasse and only ventured out on his own in 1953. An obituary notice in *The Times* observed that the designer's hallmark was "perfectly cut and structured clothes". Impeccably tailored suits were his forte; when he retired in 1971, it was not because he was short of orders but because he could no longer find tailoring staff to meet his rigorous standards. Thereafter, he worked as a design consultant for Marks & Spencer. While Michael Donnellan occasionally made visits back to Ireland (on one of these in 1954 he gave early encouragement to a young Ib Jorgensen, then a student at the Grafton Academy of Dress Design), he continued to make England his home until he died in 1985. His obituarist in the *Glasgow Herald* quoted him remarking, "All this talk of the lovely countryside. When you have escaped from a farm in Ireland, as I did, you certainly don't wish to go back to all that."

Donnellan, Cavanagh and Morton, like Molyneux before them, all opted to follow the established route to success for Irish designers in which the first step was to leave their native country. In this, they were perhaps encouraged by a want of support for Irish fashion at home. During 1950, for example, the pages of the *Irish Times* – where fashion featured no less than three times a week, on Tuesday, Thursday and Saturday – were dense with information on and photographs of the latest styles from London and Paris. What emerges from newspapers of the period is a sense that overseas work was somehow superior to that produced at home. Even when Irish fashion began to appear, it was still judged against the same set of standards. "The time has come when 'to be Irish' is not enough," pronounced the *Irish Times* in April 1953. "We are now up against international competition and although many of our fashion makers stand up well, there are still some who cannot. To these people, the 'buy Irish' slogan has been a barrier behind which they may happily shelter without making progress."

Jack Clarke

Prior to Irene Gilbert's emergence, local talents rarely received more than a passing mention. As Anne Rosse remarked in her Gilbert obituary, the prevailing view was that Irish designers were inferior to those found elsewhere and good only for making sensible, dull clothes. As if to emphasise this low opinion of indigenous ability, when Jack Clarke of Richard Alan wished to employ a designer in his company in 1949 he hired a French-Canadian called Gaston Mallet, who had previously worked with Pierre Balmain in Paris. The implication was clear; no one in Ireland was good enough for this job. Eventually, through the generous support he gave Sybil Connolly in the first years of her career as a designer, Clarke was to become one of the key figures in the creation of an Irish fashion industry.

He was among the small group of entrepreneurs in the country's clothing business who had done well in post-Independence Ireland.

Initially, he had acted as an agent for English manufacturers who wanted to sell their clothing on the other side of the Irish Sea. However in 1932, at the age of 24, he decided to set up his own company, J. N. Clarke Ltd, and opened a factory on Dublin's South William Street, in response to the Irish government's introduction of import tariffs on a wide variety of goods, including clothes. These began at 15 per cent at the start of the year and rose to 20 per cent in April, making English clothing punitively expensive to bring into the country.

The tariffs were intended to encourage local production and stimulate demand among Irish consumers for goods manufactured at home. Specifically in relation to fashion, the legislation's effect was to make Ireland even more isolated from what was happening elsewhere, particularly after the outbreak of the Second World War when the country retreated behind a policy of neutrality. Meanwhile, Jack Clarke's business, producing garments under the name Country Wear from 1944 onwards, grew rapidly. By the time the war broke out, his factory had 100 workers. He tried to keep wealthier customers up to date with international trends as best he could by opening a retail outlet carrying his clothes on Dublin's Grafton Street, called Richard Alan after the first names of his two sons. On its premises, a small dress workroom permitted the more fashion-conscious among his clientele to have couture garments made specially for them, should they so wish.

Henry White

Jack Clarke's good friends included an almost exact contemporary and potential business rival, Henry White, who began his sales career as a teenager travelling around the country with a pony and trap and a wide variety of merchandise including items of clothing. By the time he was twenty in 1929, he had opened his own clothes factory on Abbey Street in Dublin; five years later, he moved to Clarendon Street, not far from Jack Clarke's premises. Like Clarke, he was interested in offering customers stylish, well-made clothing using the best-possible fabrics and selling for the best possible price. His two sons, who took over the family business in 1977, describe how, immediately after the Second World War, their father loaded his garment van with tea and butter and drove direct to

Paris where such commodities were scarce. He exchanged them for bales of fine French cloth which, back home, were made up into coats for sale to Irish customers.

Cassidy's Fashions

A third and even more successful clothing business during this period was Cassidy's Fashions, established in Dublin by Laurence Cassidy in 1919. Forty years after its foundation, the company employed over 700 people in its three factories and four shops, where the clothes were sold under the name of Hetty Models. It is typical of the period that the workforce at Cassidy's included no designers but instead specialised in producing imitations of what was being offered by the principal fashion names in London and Paris. Just as many Irish builders even today do not necessarily employ an architect, so clothing manufacturers then did not appear to appreciate the merits – and advantages – of a fashion designer. Even quite recently, a report produced in December 1989 for the Department of the Taoiseach, on the likely impact of a single European market on the Irish clothing and textile businesses, felt obliged to point out that "product design must be given a generally higher priority in company strategy, at least equal in importance to other management functions".

The importance of good design in achieving success as a clothing manufacturer was obvious to some businessmen such as Jack Clarke (even if he initially believed that the creators of good design could only be found elsewhere) but not to many others.

A greater appreciation of what the designer could offer was only starting to emerge by this time. A week after reporting on Irene Gilbert's first fashion show, the *Irish Times* carried a long feature on dress-designing as a career option. Readers interested in pursuing such work were advised to look for a job as a designer-cutter with a clothing firm. "1950 is a most convenient date, " Elizabeth McCrum confirms, "but of course nothing happens in a vacuum. The features that would lead to the strength of Irish fashion were in place – the fabrics, the textiles, the embellishment skills were all there but it took a group of home-based designers to kick-start the industry." The moment was ripe, evidently, for Irish fashion to set up in business and gain attention for itself.

The 1950s are not as a rule remembered with much affection in Ireland. Because the succeeding decade was so full of verve and initiative, the fifties tend to be perceived as a period in which creativity was crushed or at the very best not encouraged. Patrick Kavanagh's 1952 pronouncement that, ever since Independence, "there has been a decline in vitality" certainly appears to be true in the face of key statistics from the time. Between 1951 and 1961, for example, over 400,000 Irish men and women left their native country to look for work elsewhere. By the start of the 1960s, the Republic's population was actually smaller than it had been when Independence was first achieved forty years earlier. In 1957 alone, the figure for emigration reached 54,000, a record, and 78,000 people were registered as unemployed, another record. Between 1955 and 1957, Ireland was the only country in the western world where the total volume of goods and services consumed fell rather than rose.

The times were hardly auspicious for the emergence of a vibrant new industry, and yet there were signs that fresh creativity was stirring. In the field of fashion, this translated into more jobs and greater demand for Irish clothing. As early as January 1950, the *Irish Times* noted that "the dollar-earning capacity of well-made Irish clothes is considerable. America and Canada are willing to take as much as certain Irish manufacturers can send them". These expectations of economic potential were soon realised. In 1958, the annual Coras Tráchtála [Export Board] report could remark that one of the previous year's most interesting developments "has been the sharp increase in exports of made-up garments"; in that twelve-month period, the value of overseas women's wear sales rose from £458,000 to £788,000. But, the same report pointed out, "where made-up clothing is concerned, fabric quality, styling, sizing, finish, presentation and price are essential to success."

It is interesting to note that the designers primarily responsible for achieving that success were women, in an age when business was almost totally male-dominated. "The explanation for this might lie in the importance of Irish fabrics and the way these might be embellished," Elizabeth McCrum proposes. "Patchwork, lace, crochet, tweeds; all were either made by women, designed by women or appreciated by women. So, although one can't, of course, give an absolute answer, there is a sense in which women would innately understand better the qualities of indigenous fabrics." There were, it is true, a small number of men working in the Irish fashion industry during the 1950s; the two best-known were Nicholas O'Dwyer, who for a number of years had his own shop on Suffolk Street, and Raymond Kenna. The latter occupied premises in Dublin at 56 Merrion Square which later, in 1998, were opened as a fashion outlet by designer Louise Kennedy.

Irish tweeds

Kenna was particularly admired for his finely tailored suits, often manufactured in beautifully coloured handwoven Irish tweed. An *Irish Times* review of his autumn/winter 1953 collection observed that while the clothes "may be said to show signs of continental influence", the consistent use of Donegal tweeds for suiting and coats gave this designer's work a distinctly Irish character. After his spring/summer show in January 1955, the American fashion trade journal *Women's Wear Daily* commented that Raymond Kenna was "making attractive use of domestic Irish fabrics" while the *Manchester Guardian's* fashion writer especially liked his jackets "lined with bright satin picking up a fleck of colour in the tweed".

That same month, the *Irish Times* reported: "Because of the renewed interest in tweed as a fashionable cloth, sales of Donegal tweed at home and abroad have more than doubled." One Dublin retailer said his own sales to the United States and to American visitors had grown by more than two hundred per cent over the previous twelve months. In response to this fresh demand, Gaeltarra Éireann, the state-sponsored manufacturing organisation, arranged to build a new tweed mart at Glencolumbkille, County Donegal where much of the fabric originated.

Tweed's popularity during the 1950s was due in large measure to its rediscovery and reinvention by Irish designers such as Irene Gilbert who, from the very start, incorporated it into every collection. But the tweed used for women's clothes was somewhat different from the traditional material which had been produced until then; in particular, it was of a lighter weight and came in brighter colours than hitherto. Gilbert would travel to the weaving mills of Donegal to inspect shades and weights personally, and it is an indication of the immense trouble she always took over her work that on one occasion, she brought a bunch of dried hydrangea

Howard Temple of Magee's in Donegal still remembers visits by Irene Gilbert in search of tweeds in a colour and weight to suit her requirements. Here a Donegal tweed is used for a dress and jacket from her spring/summer 1962 collection. In a shade of pale green, the jacket has short cape sleeves and a tie of white piqué threaded around the neckline.

Sybil Connolly used to insist she had almost single-handedly given new life to traditional Irish crafts, but other Irish designers also recognised their appeal. Irene Gilbert, for example, often used familiar materials in a fresh way, as with this blouse and skirt in cream handcrochet from her spring/summer 1962 collection. For the sake of customer respectability, both items were mounted on net.

flowers to the Avoca Handweavers in County Wicklow so that the tweed produced could be of precisely the same colour.

Irene Gilbert

In 2000, half a century after she showed her first collection of clothes, Irene Gilbert is far less known in Ireland than ought to be the case. A reluctant self-publicist, she was intensely shy and tended to value her privacy – not necessarily the most helpful qualities when working in a profession which has always appreciated exhibitionism. Designer Pat Crowley, who worked for Gilbert from 1960 until she opened her own business in 1968, says her former employer "was very secretive and very erratic to work with. She was terribly shy and tended to dump people, customers, with me to look after."

Irene Gilbert divulged few details about her personal life. She had been born in Thurles, County Tipperary probably around 1910 and attended Alexandra College in Dublin, followed by a brief period at a finishing school in Brussels. In a 1963 interview, she explained that while her father was Irish, her mother came from Yorkshire, "which is a very good combination for the particular job I am in, because I have the key qualities of the Celt if you like, with the practical, down-to-earth, feet-on-the-ground attitude of the Yorkshire woman." It would appear fashion was always Irene Gilbert's keenest interest; by the age of five, she was making clothes for her dolls and later on for herself. At 12, when the rest of the Gilbert family were at the races, she found a cotton dress that her mother had cut out but not made-up; by the time her parents came home, she had finished the garment and wore it proudly to school. In her late teens, she took a job in Dublin running a clothes shop called Femina's on Wicklow Street, but after a year she decided to learn some more practical skills.

She went to London, where she found a place with a court dressmaker. "We made for the top society level," she recalled. "For the nobility, for Ascot, for parties, for balls...I started at 9 in the morning and never finished before 8 or 9 at night. I was paid £3 a week and no overtime." Irene Gilbert always maintained that this kind of tough, practical apprenticeship was the best training any aspiring designer could have. And yet, curiously enough, she never "designed" clothes in the way this term would be understood today. There were, for example, no preliminary sketches of work but instead – as Sybil Connolly was also to do – she worked directly with the cloth. In an appreciation written after her death, Pat Crowley remembered how Irene Gilbert "would create on a stand with a piece of fabric which would become 'Painting the Clouds', draped and ready to go to Ascot on a titled lady". Thirty years before this appreciation, while the designer was still alive, an *Irish Times* profile of Irene Gilbert quoted her as saying "the fabric itself will suggest the way it should be treated", and noted how she would hang material on a stand and then take up her scissors. When the dress was completed, it was handed to her head fitter who marked out the lines clearly in cotton thread before taking the whole garment apart and cutting out a pattern from the different pieces.

Irene Gilbert's clothes demonstrated an abundance of technical skill; a ruby velvet evening dress was noteworthy for the exclusion from its form of all superfluous seams, with only a handful of panels used in the skirt. By contrast, her spring 1959 collection included a mustard tweed suit given surface interest thanks to double-welted seaming on both the jacket and skirt. Nothing escaped her attention, and she once remarked of her clothes, "Some people say they are so well finished they could be worn inside out."

After working almost five years for the London house, in 1935 Irene Gilbert married for the first time and, as was the norm at the time, seems to have given up her job. During the Second World War, she was employed by British Intelligence. In the mid-1940s, her marriage over, she returned to Ireland for a holiday and decided to stay in her native country. A second marriage to an Irish ex-naval officer also ended in divorce, and until her retirement she lived alone in a mews house off Northumberland Road. In 1947 she opened a shop on South Frederick Street in Dublin, stocking hats created by herself and clothes from British and French designers. It was only after the May 1950 show at Jammet's restaurant that she began to make dresses and suits for other women, and to show collections twice-yearly that were invariably well-received. A July 1953 review in the *Irish Times* of her latest line called it "essentially a collection of taste with emphasis upon uncluttered line and fine fabrics". In the same newspaper twelve years later, Terry Keane

Details such as the curving lines of welted seams seen on this coat and sleeveless dress were typical of Irene Gilbert's work. She relished technical challenges of this kind, given an added difficulty here since the fabric is a fine silk crepe. For an example of her attention to detail, look at the wonderful arabesque patterned lining just visible inside the coat.

enthused about Irene Gilbert's "ravishing collection, which showed yet again that in the world of haute couture there are no substitutes for the three fundamentals: good taste, impeccable tailoring and beautiful materials".

Irene Gilbert's clothes possessed an abundance of all three. She was never a particularly original designer but her judgement and understanding of a client's needs were flawless. And her clientele was certainly most prestigious. In addition to Anne, Countess of Rosse – described by the designer on one occasion as "a most fashionable woman; when I make something for her it combines the best of both our ideas" – she also regularly designed clothes for Lady Ursula Vernon (who together with her husband invested in the designer's business and permitted it to grow), the Countess Fitzwilliam, the Marchionesses of Headfort and Sligo, the Viscountess de Vesci and Lady Hemphill. Thanks to their support, in 1960 she was able to transfer her salon from South Frederick Street to elegant premises at 117 St Stephen's Green, where she employed a staff of over thirty women. She was a perfectionist and insisted on the highest possible standards. "It was heart-breaking at first," she was to remember. "At night I used to sit down and unpick all the work the girls had done and do it all over again."

Her favourite fabric was tweed, which she bought from a number of sources including Carberry's of Cork ("whom I find wonderfully co-operative," she said at the time), McNutt's of Donegal and the Avoca Handweavers. Often she would ask the mills to let her have balls of yarn in the colours of the tweeds and she would crochet this yarn to make yokes on dresses or over blouses to wear with her suits. Alternatively, she would darn tweeds with their own yarns at the hem and neckline. Reviews from the period highlight her skill with this Irish fabric. "Irene Gilbert proved herself a master in the handling of tweed in suits, coats and ensembles," commented Virginia Pope in the *New York Times*. "The fabrics of beautiful quality and delectable tonalities were all hand-woven…In the handling of dress fabrics, the Irish designer showed a skilled hand that recalled the technique of the great Vionnet in the use of biased cuts." But Irene Gilbert also sourced material from French and Italian mills and was keenly interested in new fibres; a July 1953 *Irish Times* review of her latest collection remarks on the inclusion of acetate satins for the second time that year.

ABOVE Irene Gilbert had few overseas clients, preferring to concentrate on her substantial domestic business, but in the early 1960s she began to export to the United States. A high-profile international customer was Princess Grace of Monaco, shown here wearing an Irene Gilbert hand-embroidered net evening dress in 1968, the year before the designer announced her retirement.

LEFT One of Irene Gilbert's favourite materials was Carrickmacross lace, which she used to spectacular effect in her evening wear. This dress, 'Stormclouds', is entirely produced from hand-made lace and helps to confirm her reputation as a intense romantic.

For evening wear, she often used lace and net – a lavish dress in these materials was made by Irene Gilbert in the mid-1960s for Princess Grace of Monaco, one of the designer's few high-profile overseas clients.

From the early 1960s onwards, Irene Gilbert began to produce not just couture but also ready-to-wear clothing, and this was available for export. By 1963, the domestic market had come to account for less than forty per cent of her business, with the United States and Canada taking up much of the rest. Pat Crowley remembers being sent to New York to sell Irene Gilbert's collection to American buyers because the designer was too ill-at-ease to do so herself. These trips included other designers such as Neilli Mulcahy, as well as manufacturers like Jack Clarke and Henry White. Although Irene Gilbert may not have cared to acknowledge the fact, she owed much of her American business to the pioneering work carried out across the Atlantic by Sybil Connolly. The two women do not seem to have acknowledged one another's existence. "There was certainly no affinity between them," Pat Crowley confirms, adding that "although Irene had more talent and more feeling for fashion, the bottom line is that she didn't have Sybil's drive."

Taken by photographer Mike Bunn towards the end of her life, this picture shows Sybil Connolly at her most regal. Although famed for her charm, the designer could be intimidating to those who did not know her. Sybil Connolly's personal style, like the clothes she designed, altered very little over a period of some forty years.

Sybil Connolly

Whatever about her abilities as a designer – and these were perhaps less great than she liked to imagine – Sybil Connolly was never less than a consummate marketer of her own work. This should come as no surprise since, for more than a decade before she produced her first public collection, she had worked as manager of the Richard Alan shop in Dublin. In November 1957, the American *Saturday Evening Post* carried a long feature in which it described how "American department store executives find themselves charmed by Sybil's smiling hazel eyes and, at the end of a delightful conversation, discover that they have been face to face with an astute saleswoman. Sybil has proved herself repeatedly an expert at the Invisible Sell." Throughout her life, the designer was notoriously charming. Fashion writer Gabrielle Williams, in a posthumous notice for the Adam's sale catalogue of

Sybil Connolly's possessions in November 1998, wrote: "her charm was faultless and alarming. She was not only a great designer, she was also a great opportunist, seizing the moment unhesitatingly."

Sybil Connolly was able to seize her moment with such confidence because she had first gone through a long, tough period of training. She was born in Wales in January 1921, of an Irish father and a Welsh mother. By her mid-teens she was living in County Waterford, but her interest in clothes meant that at the age of seventeen she was apprenticed to a London dressmaking company run by two Irish brothers, Jim and Comerford Bradley. In her later years, she would recall holding pins at fittings for Queen Mary in Bradley's where, she said, the volume of business, especially from English debutantes, meant there were no fewer than ninety-eight fitting rooms.

The outbreak of war inevitably brought a reduction in demand for debutante dresses and by 1940 Sybil Connolly was back in Ireland, and given a job by Jack Clarke at his Richard Alan shop. Here she remained, unknown to the general public, for the next thirteen years until it was time for her to emerge as a designer. Novelist Kate O'Brien was to write in 1960 that she had seen Sybil Connolly wearing a dress of her own design at a dance in Dublin's Gresham Hotel in 1946, but one of the very first people to spot and encourage the designer's talent was the late Sheila, Lady Dunsany. In an interview shortly before her death in July 1999, she remembered visiting Richard Alan's in 1951 "to buy the inevitable little black dress and I didn't like anything I saw there except what she (Sybil Connolly) was wearing which she had designed herself. I had one made and when I wore it, lots of people said how nice it was and went to her themselves." At this date, Sybil Connolly was still manageress of the Richard Alan shop, and the French-Canadian Gaston Mallet was responsible for designing Jack Clarke's collections. It was only when Mallet left at short notice in 1952 that she was given her opportunity to be recognised as a fashion designer. Suddenly, she was invited by Jack Clarke to produce the next season's range for his company.

Sybil Connolly was thirty-one when she produced her first collection and clearly knew by then exactly what effect she wanted to make. She was later to claim that prior to her arrival on the Irish fashion stage, local fabrics had been neglected – "I felt like a voice

Irish tweed manufacturers went to extraordinary lengths to assist the country's designers during the mid-century. Typical of the fabrics they handwove, often in very short lengths, is this soft-shouldered cardigan coat in blue tufted tweed worn with a more finely-woven tweed pencil-line dress, from Sybil Connolly's autumn/winter 1961 collection.

in the wilderness," she said of her efforts to promote tweed and linen – but this was obviously not the case; Irene Gilbert and Raymond Kenna were also using these materials in their collections. However, Sybil Connolly certainly brought them to greater prominence than before and she also skilfully adapted traditional Irish vernacular dress to suit the contemporary couture market. The red flannel petticoats of Connemara, for example, were recreated as billowing quilted evening skirts, twinned in time-honoured fashion with white cambric blouses and black shawls. Sophisticated redeployment of old forms was to be her forte.

Irish linen

There was no Irish fabric overlooked by Sybil Connolly, but the one most associated with her is linen. She took what was rapidly becoming a moribund material for clothing and gave it a fresh vitality. Discovering bolts of fine handkerchief linen in a Northern Irish factory, she had this folded into fine pleats and then made into dresses and skirts. Nine yards of linen were required to produce one yard of finished material; one of her earliest successes was a dress called "First Love" which contained more than five thousand pleats. Rather like the early 20th-century Venetian designer Mario Fortuny's pleated silk dresses, the great merit of Sybil Connolly's clothes was that they were extremely hard-wearing. *Harper's Bazaar* noted in June 1958 that a Connolly pleated linen skirt "will pack into a small duffel bag and emerge unscathed". Even today, her dresses can be rolled up into a ball and, with just a shake, will resume their shape. But she used linen in other imaginative ways, most famously for a summer dress called "Kitchen Fugue" in 1954 – its full skirt was made from lengths of traditional striped linen tea towels.

Dynamic and hard-working at self-promotion, Sybil Connolly still needed assistance to achieve the international success she would enjoy by the mid-1950s. Two women were of particular assistance to her. One was Sheila Dunsany who, on a 1952 trip to Philadelphia to stay with millionaire Henry McIlhenny (owner of Glenveagh Castle in Co Donegal), brought a collection of Connolly clothes with her and took orders from Americans who admired the pieces. The designer's other great supporter was the Dalkey-born editor of *Harper's Bazaar* in the United States, Carmel Snow, generally regarded as the most powerful force in international fashion during the 1940s and 1950s. Having "discovered" Sybil Connolly, she offered her unwavering loyalty thereafter. Maura Teissier, nee Boylan, who became Sybil Connolly's house model in 1954, remembers that when the editor of *Harper's Bazaar* decided to devote twelve pages of an issue to British fashion, she insisted four of these be given over to Ireland which, in effect, meant Sybil Connolly.

Carmel Snow gave an enormous boost to Sybil Connolly's career when, in July 1953, she persuaded a group of American fashion journalists and buyers to accompany her to Ireland. In her 1960 book of memoirs, *In My Fashion*, the former editor of American *Vogue*, Bettina Ballard, wrote that "Ireland was a completely unexpected centre for fashion for everyone but Carmel Snow. We were drawn en-masse to Dublin by the personable, milk-skinned Irish charmer named Sybil Connolly who showed a small collection made of Irish tweeds and linens in Dunsany Castle and bewitched us all into buying models or filling our editorial pages with them." Her friendship with its chatelaine meant Sybil Connolly was able to stage a fashion show, followed by dinner for her American visitors, in Dunsany Castle, Co Meath. Photographer Richard Dormer also used the house and its grounds for a shoot of Connolly's clothes, and one picture – showing model Ann Gunning in a full-length red

Sybil Connolly excelled at creating dramatic evening wear; the piece which made her name in the United States in 1953 was a lavish dinner dress called 'First Love'. Dating from summer 1956, this strapless evening dress is made of fabrics such as lace and silk taffeta, given still more impact by strongly contrasting colours and details like the cluster of silk flowers on the skirt.

Kinsale cape and white crochet evening dress – made the cover of *Life* magazine in August 1953 under the heading "Irish invade Fashion World". Inside the magazine were further photographs and a generous appraisal of Sybil Connolly's work.

Wisely, she decided to capitalise on this publicity by travelling with her collection to the United States where she made another life-long friend, Eleanor Lambert, doyenne of American fashion publicists. The latter later remembered that on that first transatlantic trip, Sybil Connolly "was a smash hit in America as soon as she arrived. Her charm seemed to diffuse throughout the country. Everything about her was so glamorous and wonderful. She was almost alone in Irish fashion; she brought over a feeling of it as an entity in itself." Sybil Connolly's astounding charm was matched by her energy. After that first visit to the United States in September 1953, she travelled there twice yearly, taking a new collection with her to be shown to buyers and members of the press.

Her American clientele was to include representatives of the country's wealthiest families including the Mellons, Rockefellers and Duponts. Film actresses such as Merle Oberon, Rosalind Russell, Elizabeth Taylor, Dana Wynter and Julie Andrews also bought her dresses. Most famously, when Jacqueline Kennedy sat for her official White House portrait to artist Aaron Shikler in 1970, she wore a Sybil Connolly pleated linen dress. By the time she was profiled in the *Saturday Evening Post* in November 1957, three-quarters of Sybil Connolly's gross earnings (then estimated at $500,000 per annum) originated in sales to the United States. However, she also set her sights even further afield; thanks to a friendship with newspaper magnate Frank Packer, she made two heavily publicised visits to Australia in October 1954 and August 1957 during which a series of fashion shows was staged.

In the late 1950s, she was employing around 100 women, half of them working from their own homes where they wove tweed or hand-made lace. One of the reasons for the appeal of Sybil Connolly's clothes to the American market was their romantic character; another was their relative cheapness due to the low labour costs in Ireland at the time. With unemployment at an all-time high, female workers were paid relatively low salaries. Hence, even allowing for import duties, a Sybil Connolly suit or dress could

LEFT **Sybil Connolly's genius lay in taking materials which had been produced in Ireland for generations and giving them a contemporary relevance. Here, an outfit called 'Victoria' consists of a crochet lace top with plunging neckline, worn above a high-waisted pleated linen skirt. The outfit's Irish credentials are established by the inclusion of such details as the elk's head on the wall behind.**

Simple and original, this pale yellow dinner dress is typical of Sybil Connolly's work with pleated handkerchief linen. Darted to fit the body, its only decoration is the double layer of puffed and capped short sleeves. These dresses continued to be her most popular and best-selling work for decades.

be sold in New York for less than its equivalent from elsewhere in Europe. A strapless pleated linen evening dress, for example, was available in spring 1954 for $300. Three years later, prices had barely risen, with $130 being charged for a Connolly day dress and $180 for a custom-tailored suit.

For the rest of the decade after her public debut in 1952, her career seemed to be in a steady and invincible ascent as she combined the skills of a designer with well-honed business awareness and a sharp eye for publicity. It became customary for the international press to cover not just her own twice-yearly collections but those of others such as her rival at home, Irene Gilbert. A *Women's Wear Daily* report for January 1955 noted that while American buyers "are here primarily for the Sybil Connolly opening", they were also looking at work by the likes of Raymond Kenna and the young Neilli Mulcahy. But as the decade progressed, fundamental changes began to be felt. The Irish economy improved and prices charged by outworkers rose. In addition, tastes failed to remain constant and Sybil Connolly's extravagantly romantic ballgowns fell from favour.

In February 1954, the *Daily Telegraph's* fashion correspondent Winefride Jackson had presciently observed of Sybil Connolly that "it remains to be seen, after the fuss and the furore has died down, just what place she will eventually occupy in fashion". That eventual place proved to be less exalted than once appeared to be the case. In November 1959, Sybil Connolly told the *Washington Post* that all good women designers "know that good fashion does not need to change". In fact, fashion is completely dependent on constant change and, by failing to notice the transient nature of the industry in which she worked, the designer unwittingly ensured that – even though she remained in business until her death in May 1988 – Sybil Connolly's career essentially ended when the 1950s did.

As for Irene Gilbert, evidently she had a better understanding than her rival of the fundamental changes taking place in fashion during the 1960s. Inexpensive ready-to-wear supplanted labour-intensive couture as the industry's driving force and for old-school designers like Gilbert, the shift in direction was too hard to make. When she announced her retirement in February 1969, it was noted in the *Irish Times* that "unlike other Irish designers, Miss Gilbert has not extended her business to any extent to mass production marketing". With the number of private clients interested and able to buy her work diminishing, she chose to quit the business and moved to Malta. Later she settled in the English town of Cheltenham where she died in August 1985. Because she retired so long ago and then left Ireland, Irene Gilbert has almost been forgotten in the history of Irish fashion. But the industry owes her a substantial debt. After all, its origins lie in her decision to show a handful of her own designs at Jammet's in May 1950.

Ireland's Georgian architecture acted as a source of inspiration for Sybil Connolly – her spring/summer 1954 collection, for example, was based on 18th century plasterwork, and she often used Dublin streets as a backdrop for shoots. Here, a three-quarter length black coat with outsize patch pockets and a black and white checked dress from autumn/winter 1961 are photographed on Upper Mount Street, not far from her Merrion Square home.

Unlike its equivalents in other countries, Irish fashion has always been heavily dependent on exports. As designer Paul Costelloe explains, "The biggest problem in Ireland is that the home market is so small. Americans can survive on domestic business alone but we only have a population of around four million so you have to go into exports." Irish fashion could not be sustained by the domestic market alone; the number of customers who could afford to spend large sums of money on clothes was always small and although the country has grown more affluent since the 1950s, the importance of overseas orders remains as strong as ever. What has altered is the designers' choice of preferred market; in the 1950s and early 1960s, the United States rather than Britain, our nearest neighbour, was repeatedly targeted by Irish clothing companies.

There were a number of reasons for this. One is that the authority charged with encouraging overseas trade, Coras Tráchtála, which had been set up by the government in 1951, tended to concentrate its energies on the American market. Another is the natural and long-standing affinity between the two countries. "I think America was important for Irish designers because it so patently loved what they were producing that it gave them confidence," Elizabeth McCrum remarks. "Although there were probably greater exports to the UK than to the States, it was success in America that got noticed back home. And American clients were extraordinarily loyal; they took up a designer and stayed with him or her. So America was less important perhaps in economic than in PR terms."

The distinctly ethnic character of Irish fashion at the time tended to be met with particular critical success among American journalists, who warmed to every item suggestive of an unspoilt rural world in contrast to their own. In fact, Americans were often more encouraging of this approach than were Irish journalists. Early in her career Sybil Connolly was mocked by, among others, Myles na Gopaleen in his *Irish Times* "Cruiskeen Lawn" column for what was perceived to be a "stage Irish" approach to clothes. "I can only say that I know Donegal personally, so to speak, and am surprised," he wrote in July 1954, after the designer had been quoted enthusing about the delights of peasant life in north-west Ireland. But she retorted, "This is a terribly competitive business. Unless Ireland can produce something distinctive, she will get nowhere."

Disparaging the British who had failed to respond with sufficient enthusiasm to her work at the start, Sybil Connolly announced in 1957, "America made me. Americans will always have first claim to my production." It was a statement which could have been made with equal conviction by any number of Irish designers and clothing manufacturers at the time. Coras Tráchtála began to organise regular promotions of Irish fashion and design in New York and other major American cities such as Chicago, Boston and Philadelphia. Typical of the success achieved by this strategy was the month-long "Pride of Ireland" celebration hosted in October 1963 by New York department store Lord & Taylor, which had invested in more than $1 million worth of Irish goods including almost every major fashion company. Lord & Taylor's particular interest in Irish clothing had been developed by the manager of its "Country Clothes" division, buyer Virginia "Jimmie" Booth, who had first travelled to Ireland on a buying trip in 1954 and was a regular visitor thereafter. "There is a sense that the big American department stores such as Lord & Taylor were staffed by the same young enthusiastic people as Irish designers themselves," Elizabeth McCrum remarks.

Some Irish companies waited to be offered assistance by Coras Tráchtála but others took their own initiatives. Jack Clarke of Richard Alan, for example, went on an American fact-finding mission as early as 1947, holding the first promotion of his work the following year at New York department store Abercrombie and Fitch. Thereafter he arranged regular trips to New York where between seventy and eighty pieces from his current Country Wear collection would be shown to members of the local press and buyers. And yet, for all the attention paid to the American market, it never managed to secure a large part of the Irish export business. Figures for clothing sales overseas in 1957 show that out of a total of £2,689,000, a mere £113,000 went to the United States, and more than ninety per cent went to Britain. Ten years later, exports of Irish clothing to American stockists had risen to be worth £1,250,000, but demand from British retailers by this date had also correspondingly increased.

By then, two factors were encouraging greater trade with our nearest neighbour. One was the removal of the tariffs which, since the 1930s, had discouraged the development of business links

When Neilli Mulcahy showed her first solo collection, she set it in the family home, Lissenfield, in the Dublin suburb of Rathmines. It included this knee-length red velour coat, with a wide-brimmed hat made by milliner Elizabeth Fanagan who shared premises with her in South Frederick Street and collaborated with her for many years. The photograph was taken in the grounds of Lissenfield.

between the two countries. The Anglo-Irish Free Trade Agreement, signed in December 1965 and effective from July 1st the following year, abolished all import duties on Irish goods into Britain and helped Irish clothing manufacturers to expand into their most convenient market. But that process had already begun in April 1964 with the first of what were to become annual Irish Export Fashion Fairs, aimed specifically at international markets. Organised by Coras Tráchtála and held in Dublin's Intercontinental Hotel, the debut fair attracted around 630 overseas buyers and 80 non-Irish journalists; visitors from Britain naturally predominated in both categories and Irish fashion's dependence on this market quickly became apparent. The fourth Irish Export Fashion Fair, for example, saw orders decline from the previous year's figure of £1.1 million to £750,000. The explanation for this drop was a decrease in the number of British buyers because their own businesses were going through a temporary slump. In future, fluctuations in the British economy would have a direct impact on Irish fashion exports. This dependence on Britain and the problems it can cause continue to the present day.

Kay Petersen

In 1967, the Coras Tráchtála annual report noted that "one of the chief prerequisites for continued export expansion in the apparel industries is further improvement in design and styling. Irish firms are already meeting the demands of overseas buyers for better and more up-to-date styles." Nevertheless, many of the most successful designers of the period continued to offer clothing which both in fabric and styling could only have come out of an Ireland still enamoured of its traditions and history. An obvious instance of this tendency to look back could be seen in the work of Kay Petersen who, during the 1960s, had a company and a shop on Dublin's Dawson Street called Anna Livia.

A year before his death, the poet and critic Louis MacNeice wrote a feature on Ireland for the *New Statesman* in June 1962 in which he described one of Petersen's fashion shows. Held, naturally enough, on Bloomsday, it featured designs in Irish tweed bearing such names as "Finnegan" and "Martello". Having seen the designer's work with brilliantly-hued tweeds MacNeice – not a man known for his fashion expertise – was moved to comment "Kay Petersen has stood the concept 'tweedy' on its head". At the time of the first Irish Export Fashion Fair this designer, who was to work with Thomas Wolfangel in the 1970s, announced, "my look is completely indigenous to Ireland," although adding "I hope it has an international appeal". For a time it would have, but over-emphasising a garment's ethnic origins was always going to be risky in a market as subject to rapid changes of taste as fashion. "Irish" style could be in vogue one season but out the next. The designers who enjoyed the most enduring careers tended to take advantage of Irish materials and traditional forms but not be limited by them.

Neilli Mulcahy

Neilli Mulcahy's work shows that it was possible to be both overtly Irish and yet have an international appeal. Born in Dublin in 1925, she was the daughter of General Richard Mulcahy, former Commander-in-Chief of the Irish army and a minister in successive governments. Because there was a keen family interest in education, she initially studied science at university but left after a year and investigated various other options before eventually taking classes at the Grafton Academy of Dress Design where, after graduation, she taught for a year and a half. While it soon became clear that she would open her own business, she chose to work for six months in the Paris atelier of Jacques Heim, a couturier now remembered primarily for having first featured the bikini in a 1946 collection. While in Paris, Neilli Mulcahy perfected her sewing skills; she later remembered making thirty-four button holes on a shantung dress in a single day because such work had to be completed in one sitting so as to ensure the style of the worker's hand remained the same.

In October 1952, at the age of 27, she opened premises in her own name at 30 South Frederick Street, where she remained for eighteen years. For some years, she shared the South Frederick Street building with a friend, the milliner Elizabeth Fanagan, who made hats to complement Neilli Mulcahy's clothes. At first, the designer did not hold her own fashion shows but exhibited items for competition in the annual National Fashion Parades, organised

Grace O'Shaughnessy, one of Ireland's best-known models from the late 1950s and 1960s, here wears an outfit probably from late in Neilli Mulcahy's career, displaying the contemporary move away from formal clothing to a more casual style. Even though the styling of the cropped pants and hooded jacket is modern, the latter's fabric is traditional, a green and grey handwoven Donegal tweed with insets of grey top-stitched flannel.

in Dublin each May by the National Agricultural and Industrial Development Association (NAIDA). The quality of her work was immediately recognised; in the 1953 NAIDA show, she was chosen as a prizewinner by Elsa Schiaparelli, the visiting judge. Early reviews of her clothes often refer to the glamour of her evening wear, with one much-photographed example featuring tiered layers of white lawn below a tightly-boned bodice in bottle-green taffeta.

When Neilli Mulcahy held her first solo fashion show in January 1955, the venue was her family home, Lissenfield in Rathmines. Reviews of this event make mention of tweed which was thereafter one of her favourite fabrics; the *Irish Press's* fashion correspondent of the time picked up the overtly Irish character of her work, noting how "green was the predominating colour of the collection and tweed the important material". However, "clever cutting made rather heavyweight tweeds hang well in boxy jackets". Two years later, Caroline Mitchell in the *Irish Times* was also writing about Neilli Mulcahy's use of tweeds; in a neutral-coloured thick-knit for a suit called "Stir-About" and in a slightly lighter weight for a slim skirt combined with a low-fastening double-breasted jacket. The latter ensemble was presciently called "Aer Lingus", because in December 1963 she designed a new uniform for the Irish national airline employing a blue and fern green "darn weave" tweed from McNutt's, one of three Donegal companies regularly used by her for cloth. The other two were Malloy's and Magee's, and some tweeds also came from Avoca Handweavers in County Wicklow.

According to Elizabeth McCrum, "Neilli's strength lay in her use of heavy tweed, even in evening wear. She worked, of course, in lots of fabrics but I always think of her long, strongly-shaped evening coats and matching dresses. She had a great love of Irish tweed and wasn't afraid to use it in weights others might have shied away from." Mills would liaise closely with designers at the time to produce bolts of fabric in the colours specified. In addition, Neilli Mulcahy would sometimes buy the yarn being used for weaving and have it knitted into co-ordinating items; these might then carry printed designs to add extra surface interest to the finished work. In 1965, for example, she began to print on báinín, and two years later she presented a knitted woollen dress called "Inishmaan" which carried a print of traditional Aran stitching. Knitted fabric might also be set as panels into tweed garments.

Like many designers of the period, Neilli Mulcahy was interested in printing designs onto fabric. In 1967, she printed this Aran-knit pattern in anthracite grey onto a simple long knitted off-white shift. The dress is modelled by the designer's sister-in-law, who continued to wear it for more than twenty years.

Neilli Mulcahy always disliked extraneous details and her clothes were distinguished by their clean lines and want of fuss. Rosemarie Mulcahy models a wedding dress dating from 1967 and combining the old – worsted báinín wool – with the new, thanks to the garment's contemporary styling.

Other materials for her clothes came from Abraham's of Switzerland and Liberty's of London; the latter's designer, Michael McInerny, produced prints exclusively for her. These fabrics tended to be lighter than the tweeds and were therefore used for blouses and evening dresses.

Neilli Mulcahy was renowned for her bold use of colour. Typical examples of her work include a darted, sleeveless shift dress in apple green dating from the mid-1960s and a pale blue worsted coat lined in emerald green, this latter colour then used for a matching worsted caftan. Again, she regularly printed simple bold designs onto her pieces. Shapes were never elaborate and the finish invariably perfect, thanks to her intensive training. Her designs were practical – she once remarked "I'm very much a believer that you must have pockets" – but the evidence of skilled workmanship was usually kept well-hidden; garment closings, for example, would usually be concealed.

Neilli Mulcahy received much publicity from the American press in March 1959 when her aunt, Mrs Sean T O'Kelly, wife of the Irish president, wore the designer's clothes on an official visit to the United States. She had already been noticed by journalists crossing the Atlantic to cover the Irish collections in Dublin; a multi-coloured plaid ensemble was described by the *New York Times* as displaying "imaginative whimsy", while a year later *Women's Wear Daily* declared "she has a way with tweeds which is worth watching". Indeed, that publication continued to watch her keenly and in 1967 was carrying a report of the latest Neilli Mulcahy collection which, as usual, offered clients "every form of tweed from the very light to very bulky and lots of shades of blue".

The United States had become an important outlet for the designer's clothes by the early 1960s and, like so many other Irish designers, she made regular trips across the Atlantic to present her latest collection to American customers. In fact, in 1967 she showed her clothes on the Atlantic, while travelling to New York on board the liner *Rotterdam*. But Neilli Mulcahy remained essentially a couturier rather than a producer of ready-to-wear clothes. In 1962, along with Irene Gilbert, Ib Jorgensen and Clodagh, she founded the Irish Haute Couture Group, the aims of which were the promotion, assistance and encouragement of domestic fashion at couture level.

Seven years earlier, after her first solo show, the *Irish Times* had described how the designer "treats each client as an individual and will never repeat any garment exactly". But as the 1960s progressed, demand for clothing of this kind diminished and in 1970, after eighteen years working as a fashion designer, Neilli Mulcahy took the decision to close her business. Her South Frederick Street premises had been sold; changes in the local bye-laws meant manufacturing in that area was no longer permitted. She had six small children and, having made three trips to the United States in the previous eighteen months, she was beginning to find running a business and raising a family too much of a challenge. "And remember," she later commented, "denim and jeans came in and killed off a lot of fashion at that time." After working as a part-time fashion consultant for a number of years, she left the business altogether.

Mary O'Donnell

Mary O'Donnell, another designer of this period, is often bracketed with Neilli Mulcahy. Born in Kilcar, County Donegal, as a young child she learnt how to embroider, knit and crochet. "In fact," she says, "I could knit and read a book at the same time; I did one for the money and the other for the pleasure. It was only later in life, when I'd gone away, that I realised I had a tremendous knowledge of textiles and an appreciation of texture." By the time she was in her teens, she was also spinning and carding cloth. In 1951, at the age of 17, she emigrated to the United States and worked in a variety of jobs, none of them connected with fashion, before enrolling as a student at the Traphagen Academy of Dress Design in New York. She also spent some time in the city's Bergdorf Goodman department store working in the alterations department.

Eventually, she achieved her ambition and was offered a position with the American couturier Mainbocher – now remembered for making the Duchess of Windsor's wedding dress in June 1937 – where she stayed for the next two and a half years. "He was very inventive," she later said of Mainbocher. "He bought materials from all over the world but he would always do something different with them. He might layer three chiffons for

One of Mary O'Donnell's first customers in her shop on Dawson Street, Dublin in 1963 was the artist Sean O'Sullivan (whose portrait of Sybil Connolly now hangs in the National Gallery of Ireland). He bought one of the designer's patchwork skirts for his daughter and shortly afterwards made this pencil sketch of Mary O'Donnell.

TOP Sophisticated but traditional romanticism was always Mary O'Donnell's hallmark. In this ensemble from the late 1960s, a skirt of handwoven silk taffeta produced in Dublin's Liberties district is combined with a hand-crocheted sleeveless top through which ribbons have been slotted. The laden Irish dresser emphasises the designer's interest in her own country's craft skills.

ABOVE Her work often had a rustic charm, but Mary O'Donnell was also perfectly able to produce cosmopolitan designs. This evening dress from 1967, made of heavy black silk and with a short black organza cape, reveals its Irish origins through the inclusion of a halter neck of hand-made crochet through which ribbon has been slotted.

depth of colour, or add ribbons or embroider it." From her time with the couture house, she believed herself forever after "brainwashed on elegance and understatement". When Mainbocher retired in 1961, Mary O'Donnell returned home and took a job with Sybil Connolly. However, in 1963, with just £100, she opened her own small premises when a shop became available at 43 Dawson Street in Dublin.

Despite her background with Mainbocher, who had a restrained, almost austere style, Mary O'Donnell's designs were always known for their exuberant romanticism. She liked to insist all her work had its origins in the craft tradition so that even pieces with a contemporary character such as a bolero jacket and cropped pants from her spring 1971 collection were made in hand-crocheted cotton. Crochet work was one of her favourite forms; typically, for a fashion show at Powerscourt House in County Wicklow in April 1966, she produced a number of pieces using this traditional Irish craft, including an evening dress of pale pink wild silk with a bodice of cream crochet slotted with ribbon, and a wedding dress made entirely of white hand crochet in a flower design with satin ribbon slotted through each flower. In a report on Irish fashion from April 1970, *The Lady* magazine carried a photograph of Mary O'Donnell's voluminous silk poplin skirt with Edwardian-style hand crocheted blouse. Poplin, first introduced into this country by Huguenot weavers in the late 17th century, was another consistent favourite in the designer's collections, along with embroidery using traditional Irish motifs.

Mary O'Donnell regularly turned to her native country's past for inspiration, and by the late 1970s she was giving her collections and fashion shows themes taken from Irish literature. The work of W.B. Yeats seems particularly to have inspired her. A fashion presentation for the Irish American Cultural Institute in Minnesota in July 1978 was themed around several of Yeats's poems so that a dress called "Coole Park" had swooping birds embroidered across its surface in recollection of the lines: "They came like swallows and like swallows went…" "I had a lot of couture shows in Dublin," she remembers. "When I was finished making the clothes, I was too tired and could never think of names to put on them. When I started, I used to give them the names of rivers and mountains, nice-sounding ones. Then I was reading Yeats's poetry and I saw 'a rose-embroidered hem', 'silk kimonos', 'had I the heavens' embroidered cloths', and I was off. I started using some of the symbolism he had in the poetry and it worked very well. It gave me an inspiration and it certainly was terrific for a show. Then I did fifteen or twenty pieces which absolutely represented the poems and I presented those several times in America."

"We are the last bastion of Celtic civilisation and our talents are largely untapped," Mary O'Donnell once said. Her own talent was for couture and inevitably the number of Irish clients she could find was limited. By 1980, at least half of her business was found in the United States where she established strong links with members of the Kennedy family; ten years before, *Women's Wear Daily* had carried a report of Mary O'Donnell's fashion show held in the garden of Senator Edward Kennedy's Washington home. Other clients included Miranda, Countess of Iveagh, Princess Grace of Monaco and Maureen O'Hara. In the mid-1970s Mary O'Donnell described her business as "basically a cottage industry" employing some 35 women working from their own homes (often in her native Donegal)

By the time this picture was taken in 1965, Tony Higgins had become the preferred photographer for Irish designers. His work kept abreast of international trends but still placed clothes in an Irish context. Here he photographed a pair of Capri pants in pale pink lace and matching sleeveless top, both by Mary O'Donnell.

Mary O'Donnell made a point of using materials from County Donegal and the north-west, where she had grown up. Here, linen has been made into a long skirt banded at the hem and embroidered with floral motifs in the lower sections, teamed with a neutral-toned silk top. Both pieces date from the mid-1960s.

and a further ten staff in her Dawson Street workrooms. In 1983 she closed her shop because "it was pretty obvious there was a winding up of couture and the future wasn't going to be there". She then ran a factory in Donegal for three years, admitting later "it was a struggle" since she was unaccustomed to the rigours of mass production. Thereafter, she alternated between Ireland and the United States, the latter being home to most of her surviving clientele.

In 1965 Ernestine Carter, fashion writer with the *Sunday Times* and an early admirer of Mary O'Donnell's work, wrote that the designer's clothes were "unashamedly pretty" with "the refreshing innocence of a long cool drink of water". They were also labour-intensive and costly to produce; in 1970, the *Irish Press* noted that one of her crochet pieces sold for £130, "putting Mary O'Donnell's clothes very decisively in the luxury bracket". As a number of other Irish designers who focused on the couture market also found, fewer and fewer women were interested in such clothes, particularly when they had such a strong ethnic character.

Clodagh O'Kennedy

Could a younger generation of customers be persuaded to wear clothes with an unquestionably Irish origin? This was the challenge posed to herself by Clodagh O'Kennedy, always known simply by her first name alone. Born in County Mayo, Clodagh was raised in the country and originally hoped either to work with horses or to paint; her parents, on the other hand, wanted her to study mathematics at Trinity College, Dublin. "None of my family had ever gone into trade," she says. "When I decided to become a designer, my mother gave me £400 and my father threw me out of the house; mind you, he took me back once he saw all the publicity I was getting for my work." Generating publicity was always Clodagh's forte; like Sybil Connolly, she knew how to produce a good story for the press. Since she was so young – just seventeen - when she first began to work as a fashion designer in the late 1950s after a very brief period in the Grafton Academy of Dress Design, she never failed to receive extensive coverage, always being referred to as "the youngest of the Irish designers". "I was certainly very

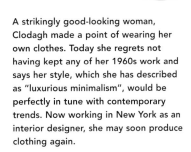

A strikingly good-looking woman, Clodagh made a point of wearing her own clothes. Today she regrets not having kept any of her 1960s work and says her style, which she has described as "luxurious minimalism", would be perfectly in tune with contemporary trends. Now working in New York as an interior designer, she may soon produce clothing again.

successful publicity-wise," she agrees. "But I was never a huge financial success. I was so dumb about finances; when my bank manager asked to see my books, I wondered why he wanted to know what I was reading."

Clodagh used traditional Irish materials such as crochet and tweed, but in a fresh way. "She was very modern in the shapes she cut," says Elizabeth McCrum. "She managed to keep the standards of couture but make it very contemporary incorporating crochet, fabric printing and different fine weaves of tweed." Clodagh designed clothes "for people

Clodagh's fashion shows were notable for her determination to leave nothing to chance. She took responsibility for every aspect of the production and, unusually for the time, made sure hair, make-up, lighting and music were all co-ordinated: "To the last hair and the most exact shade of lipstick, the models are perfectly in harmony with the dresses they are presenting" (*Irish Times*, October 1965).

like myself – in a hurry and wanting things that would work long and hard. They were people travelling, on the move, people who liked simplicity." In particular, she produced designs which were more fluid and sensual than had previously been the case in Ireland, where ladylike respectability was the norm in matters of dress. "Clodagh typifies the best in Irish fashion," remarked the *New York Daily News* in October 1965. "Here is fresh fun, superb in colour and texture….Her colours are rich and warm, her fabrics textured tweeds and wools, the line narrow and easy, the evening look casual, with a flick of Irish lace."

Clodagh herself describes her work at the time as sexy. "I believed then, as I do now, in a total look. I made the models throw away their bras. I was an early feminist. I threw out girdles which I thought were very bad for the body. " Her clothes tended to cling and fit close to the form and, again unusually for the period in Ireland, she would use not just traditional fabrics but also unfamiliar materials such as silk jersey. She was particularly noted for her body-hugging crochet dresses; "One thing I worked on more than other designers was texturing rather than patterns. I did

What distinguished Clodagh from other Irish designers was her interest in producing work with an overt sensuality. The quality has never been a strong feature of the country's fashion and is therefore all the more striking when it appears, as in this long check tweed coat trimmed with fur at the collar and cuffs and shown with a pair of matching knee-high boots.

experiment with printing on tweed, but I wasn't wild about that."

At the time of the first Irish Export Fashion Fair, the *Times* recorded the young designer as expressing a desire to make clothes "that look well and wear well and aren't gimmicky. In a shift, I like to indicate the body line so you can still see there's a woman underneath. And no frills – I don't like things stuck on for no reason." But she was not immune to the charms of surface decoration. Miranda, Countess of Iveagh, who moved to Ireland after her marriage in 1963, was a big fan of Clodagh and still has one of the designer's coats "in a lovely soft biscuity-brown tweed and she had appliquéd crochet roses around the neck". Miranda Iveagh also remembers "amazing crochet dresses. I think she made liberated clothes and had a generosity of design which was terribly exciting".

Initially, like her peers, Clodagh offered only couture clothing but she later began to produce ready-to-wear as well. Her main market was the United States where she regularly travelled with the aid of Coras Tráchtála; further American trips were made once she joined the board of the International Fashion Advisory Council, where she remained for ten years.

Because of her strongly independent nature, Clodagh had decided while still a teenager that she would always work for herself "but I tried to surround myself with the best people I could find". However, in 1972, she decided to close down her company. "I wasn't making money," she explains. "I wasn't doing well, I was divorcing, I had to pay back too much too fast and my business crashed. Also, the more I thought about it, the more I felt I had to do something stronger and less ephemeral. Fashion seemed too decorative." After spending some time in Spain, she moved to New York where she now runs an extremely successful architectural and design company in Manhattan. "I think Clodagh's retirement from fashion could be seen as the end of some sort of tradition but perhaps too much is made of her departure," Elizabeth McCrum comments. "I feel of Clodagh that she'd 'done' fashion. She'd given it her best shot and, as her subsequent career indicates, she'd a lot more interests." Before she left Ireland, Clodagh disposed of all her old material and now owns almost nothing to recall her past as a designer in Dublin.

Áine Lawlor

Because it is preoccupied with the future, fashion tends to have an extraordinarily short memory. Many of the other designers who were successful in Ireland around the same period – the late 1950s and 1960s - have now been largely forgotten. In December 1959, for example, Áine Lawlor, who had begun working as a couturier three years earlier, staged a fashion show for her many clients at the Gresham Hotel in Dublin which was one of the most talked- and written-about occasions that winter. The designer had trained at the Grafton Academy in 1949 and then worked in London with John Cavanagh for a time before returning to Dublin to teach at the Academy for a year in 1954. She then established her own label specialising in eveningwear and wedding dresses but her clothes, which often drew on Irish legends and history for their inspiration, are little remembered today.

Sheila Mullally

Then there was Sheila Mullally, who opened her own business on Dublin's Wellington Road in 1964. As an *Irish Times* review of her autumn/winter collection the following year noted, her clothes were likely to be worn as much by American as by Irish women. The same feature remarked that 85 per cent of the tweeds used by the designer were from her native country. Before setting up on her own, Sheila Mullally had worked as in-house designer for the Elizabeth James label based in Cork. Once more, the principal fabric employed in successive seasons by this company was Irish tweed, frequently in bright colours and bold check patterns.

It was only when heavy materials started to fall out of favour with consumers that long-established Irish businesses found themselves in trouble. By the mid-1960s, fashion was beginning to move decisively in a new direction. In order to survive, Irish designers needed to change the clothes they produced but also, and more importantly, they needed to reconsider their outlook on the fashion industry.

"I like fabrics with some sort of texture," Clodagh announced in 1964. "I think they're more flattering to the skin." She also believed that clothes which suggested the body beneath were more attractive than loose-fitting pieces. This tight Aran cardigan with high collar has plenty of surface texture and, at the same time, a youthful sense of style.

growth and prosperity: 1960–70

The 1960s have always enjoyed a very positive image, in stark contrast to the preceding decade. This perception arose from the new-found buoyancy of the Irish economy, even though the change actually began in 1959 with the implementation of the first Programme for Economic Expansion. Following the advice of T.K. Whitaker of the Department of Finance, the Irish government made a decision to invest heavily in industry - until then somewhat neglected in preference to agriculture - with a particular emphasis on exports. Inevitably, this was to the advantage of the clothing trade. Sales of Irish clothes stood at just over £3 million in 1958; by 1966, that figure had risen to almost £10.5 million.

American journalist Donald S. Corkery in his book *The Irish* (1968) commented, "Returning to Ireland in early 1963, it was impossible not to feel the atmosphere change or notice the many signs of modernisation. There was an unaccustomed briskness about the way Dubliners moved and a freshness of complexion which I had not seen before." That briskness and freshness may be explained in part by changing demographics. The 1966 national census showed that, compared to the figures of its predecessor five years earlier, the number of Irish people aged 15 to 29 had grown by ten per cent. Meanwhile, national income rose during the same period by 25 per cent and the number of unemployed dropped by around 30 per cent. Emigration also appeared to have been terminally arrested and the population of larger cities and towns was on the increase; in Dublin alone it grew by approximately 30 per cent. Tangible evidence of Ireland's new prosperity could be seen in the opening of the country's first shopping centre in Stillorgan, County Dublin in 1966, followed soon after by another even bigger conglomeration at Cornelscourt, also in the capital's suburbs. Young, affluent and urban; these were the attributes of the new generation. They were also the people most likely to be interested in fashion, so no wonder Ireland's industry felt particularly optimistic during the 1960s.

It is often said that men only enter a profession once this has proven its economic viability. Certainly, until the 1960s Irish fashion had been dominated by women but thereafter it started increasingly to become a male industry. Designer Richard Lewis, who himself first set up his business in 1965, notes that before that date clothing manufacturers were mostly men, but designers were mostly women. "There are more male designers now, which makes the business seem more serious and get more backing," he says. "If men go into an industry, backers or manufacturers will take it more seriously."

The Grafton Academy

Irish fashion was becoming a more professional industry largely thanks to the Grafton Academy of Dress Design, which offered aspiring fashion designers an opportunity to learn key skills such as pattern-making and cutting. Although established in 1939 by Pauline Keller (later known by her married name of Pauline Clotworthy), the Academy only started to make a major impact on Irish fashion from the 1950s onwards. Born in Dublin, Pauline Keller had attended the city's Metropolitan School of Art before going to the British Institute of Dress Design in London where her fellow students included Michael Donnellan and Hardy Amies. Returning to Ireland just before the outbreak of the Second World War, she set up her new business on the first floor of 6 St Stephen's Green in Dublin, providing a full range of skills in both dressmaking and millinery.

The Grafton Academy was the first institution of its kind in the country. Formerly, anyone who wished to become a designer had to seek work with an established fashion house and gradually learn by a mixture of keen observation and hard work; this is how both Irene Gilbert and Sybil Connolly received their initial training. Even after the Grafton Academy opened to students, many years were to pass before another fashion course was offered in Ireland; the National College of Art and Design only began its diploma in 1972, followed by a degree in 1977, while the Limerick School of Art and Design provided undergraduates with the chance to study fashion from 1973.

Pauline Clotworthy was, therefore, a fashion trailblazer. As former model Marguerite MacCurtin, who worked many times with the Academy's founder, comments, "I think she offered a necessary resource to people wanting to study fashion at a time when there was nowhere else. The subject might have been looked down upon in some quarters as slightly frivolous. Pauline was very vigorous and inspirational and way before her time." By 1945, the Academy had

For four decades, some of Ireland's best-known women bought their clothes from Ib Jorgensen. This fuschia silk cloque dress and jacket from his autumn/winter 1992 collection was ordered by the country's President at the time, Mary Robinson, who wore the outfit that autumn when she met Queen Elizabeth II on a state visit to England. Mrs Robinson's clothes from that occasion are now in Madame Tussaud's, London.

outgrown its premises on St Stephen's Green and had to move to a new site at 17/18 South Frederick Street. In 1981, it moved again to 6 Herbert Place and is now run by Pauline Clotworthy's daughter Suzanne Marr. Many of the best known names in Irish fashion began their careers with a period at the Grafton Academy, among them Neilli Mulcahy, Paul Costelloe, Richard Lewis, Pat Crowley and Louise Kennedy.

Ib Jorgensen

Probably the first male name of note to emerge from the Academy was Ib Jorgensen, who spent a year there in 1952. Born in Denmark, he was aged 14 when his family moved to Ireland after his father took up a position as advisor to the pig-farming industry then being established by the Department of Agriculture. While a student at the Academy, he won two prizes in the annual NAIDA fashion competition, judged that year by Michael Donnellan. Ib Jorgensen's clothes were shown on this occasion by his sister Hanne, who was later to become a well-known model in Ireland.

He then spent a couple of years working for the designer Nicholas O'Dwyer, who had premises on Suffolk Street. Here he both designed and perfected his pattern-cutting skills on a weekly salary of £14. But it was inevitable that Ib Jorgensen would set up his own business and in 1956, with just two members of staff, he did so in premises on South Frederick Street. Soon this was to be followed by a move to Nassau Street and 20 staff, before eventually he established himself at 24 Fitzwilliam Square with workrooms on the ground floor and a team of 45 people. Here he continued to do his own pattern-cutting, an instance of the perfectionism always evident in his finished clothes.

Ib Jorgensen's work was known for its attention to detail and immaculate fit. While still a student, Michael Mortell spent a year with him in the mid-1970s and remembers: "When I came to work for Ib Jorgensen I suddenly realised how little I knew. It was a pleasure to work for him because he was incredibly professional. I thought he was a great designer of couture. Technically, he was brilliant, he made all his own patterns and a lot of them were very complicated." In his designs, Ib Jorgensen was never particularly adventurous – "I'm a classical designer," he once said - although

ABOVE In 1967, Ib Jorgensen married Patricia Murray, a textile designer. She often produced designs for beading, appliqué and hand-painting on his garments. Photographed here in the couple's Fitzwilliam Square home, she wears an Ib Jorgensen dress, the skirt of which has been hand-painted with one of her designs showing rearing horses.

LEFT Although his clothes were often characterised by a sense of discretion, Ib Jorgensen was not afraid of making bold statements when it suited him. Such is certainly the case with this evening dress in a heavy silk crepe printed with a kinetic-style print; the fabric has been caught on one shoulder from which it falls in a Grecian manner.

the items hand-painted, appliquéd or embroidered to his wife Patricia's designs were strikingly original and much coveted. "There's always quite an element of formality about what I design," he explained in 1993, although "I make less and less really formal things."

His clothes could not be described as cheap; by the time he closed his business in February 1994, a two-piece ensemble cost in the region of £1,200, but he was always prepared to justify the prices charged. "Couture clothes are handmade," he explained to the *Irish Times* in January 1981. "The difference between my workrooms and, say, a factory is that my garment is made by one person apart from the finishing. She sees the whole garment right through the process and it is a very personal garment – that's why it is so costly." For a long time, there were plenty of women prepared to pay the high prices he charged. By the late 1970s, at the height of his success, he had shops in London and Dublin – on Sloane Street and Molesworth Street respectively – with workrooms in both cities also. So great was the demand for his clothes, especially among the racing set, that he was able to say, "At any great race meeting, the enclosures are full of my clothes. It is like a Jorgensen fashion show."

However, with the change of direction fashion began to take during the 1980s – influenced by the dominance of Japanese designers with their predilection for unstructured black clothing – Ib Jorgensen began to lose some of his favour with a market which was, in any case, growing older; in 1993, he summarised his customers as being "chic women in the 35-55 age bracket". Potential younger clientele preferred to look elsewhere for their clothes; it was only in the early 1990s that he introduced a ready-to-wear collection. His own work he described in August 1993 as "well made. I have excellent workrooms and highly-trained skilled people. They are always different but they still have a handwriting of what I am – like an artist." His fabrics were always very beautiful and in the finest yarns. Furthermore, unlike most Irish designers, he enjoyed using bright and bold prints, with many materials bought abroad.

When, after 40 years in the business, Ib Jorgensen closed down his fashion house, he blamed the government imposition of 21 per cent VAT on clothing for this decision. "There's no way I'm staying

RIGHT **Ib Jorgensen's reputation as Ireland's leading couturier was based on ensembles such as this impeccably finished suit and coat from 1967. Note how panels of the fine woven wool used for the jacket and skirt have been introduced around the collar, cuffs and hem of the coat's boldly-checked tweed. The entire outfit was ordered by Harrods for its International Room.**

on in business because it simply isn't viable…We made good money in the late '70s and early '80s but since then it's been a struggle." But pragmatism also played a part in his move away from fashion into fine art – he now runs an art gallery from his former salon on Dublin's Molesworth Street. Shortly before he showed his final collection to the public, he told the *Irish Times's* Gabrielle Williams that "Quality is disappearing". True or not, demand for quality of the kind he offered was indisputably in decline.

Thomas Wolfangel

Ib Jorgensen was not the only man to come to prominence in Ireland as a couturier during the 1960s. Another was Thomas Wolfangel, whose origins also lay outside Ireland. Born in Stuttgart, Germany, he was the son of a tailor and once explained his interest in fashion by saying "It was bred into me". He first moved to Ireland in 1957, initially working for a German clothing company in Sligo. Then he was taken on by Kay Petersen of Anna Livia before setting up on his own in the mid-1960s. Roles were reversed in 1978 when Kay Petersen came to work with Wolfangel in the boutique he had just opened on Lower Baggot Street in Dublin; more recently he has been based on Pembroke Road. Although never running as large an operation as Ib Jorgensen, Thomas Wolfangel has remained in business and continues to show a new collection every season.

His clientele is predominantly drawn from Dublin and the immediately surrounding counties; women who are looking for well-made suiting and eveningwear in sturdy fabrics. They have never sought to be taken to the wilder shores of fashion. As a review in the *Evening Press* in August 1983 commented, "No matter what the seasonal trends and fads may be, Thomas Wolfangel can always be expected to produce 'smart' clothes." The same reviewer also remarked that while she found many of his dresses rather old-fashioned, "I suppose some would call them timeless". In the 1980s, his clothes were often worn by Maeve Hillery, wife of the President of Ireland, as well as many members of the diplomatic circuit. His appeal to clients of this ilk is underlined by the annual visit Thomas Wolfangel pays to the United States,

Many of Thomas Wolfangel's most loyal customers are women who live not in Dublin but its surrounding counties such as Kildare and Meath. For them, he has always offered coats and suits in familiar fabrics and devoid of too many details which will quickly date. This button-through skirt and matching jacket trimmed in leather is typical of such work and, except perhaps for the broad shoulders, hardly suggests that it was designed as long ago as 1980.

hosting a show of his work in Washington, D.C., where there are many women prepared to invest in couture.

Despite being so long in the business, Thomas Wolfangel can still delight. His collection for autumn/winter 1999 was judged to be one of the best for some time; there was restraint in his choice of fabrics such as speckled tweeds and plain cashmeres and such comfortably familiar features of the designer's work as pintucking on coats and jackets. Among fabrics, he has consistently used Irish tweed in his work and, given his family background, his skills as a tailor are understandably strong.

ABOVE In addition to his Irish customers, Wolfangel has also maintained a loyal following in the United States where he stages a show annually, most often in Washington D.C. It is for the latter group of women that he produces eveningwear of the kind shown here in which rich fabrics rather than elaborate techniques provide the drama. The silk taffeta dress with ruched bodice and heavy brocade jacket dates from 1980.

LEFT In the mid-1980s Mari O'Leary, who has since gone on to run her own public relations business, was probably Ireland's most successful model. Here she is seen wearing a typical suit from the mid-1980s by Thomas Wolfangel. The navy wool gabardine skirt's inverted pleats and generous length reflect the concerns of his loyal customers whose tastes have tended to become more conservative with age. The matching jacket is piped in red.

Donald Davies

From the very start, tailoring has played an important role in the history of Irish fashion. The most important native fabrics, especially tweed, lend themselves to work of this kind and the climate of Ireland means that sturdy, tailored clothing will never fail to find a welcome. A streak of conservatism which has run unfailingly through Irish fashion (and, indeed, the Irish temperament) would also encourage appreciation of the merits of sensible, tailored work. However, during the 1960s an altogether more relaxed and less formal approach to dressing began to appear. For men and women alike, suiting was no longer the only option and inexpensive casual clothes, often sold in small retail outlets, began to appear. One man who was ready to take advantage of these changes in fashion was Donald Davies.

Yet another instance of an outsider who did much to enhance the reputation of Irish fashion, Donald Davies originally came from Wales, moving to Ireland just before the Second World War as the representative of an English shirt-making company. In 1955, he set up a business in Enniskerry, County Wicklow, where he lived with his family in Charleville, an exceptionally beautiful Georgian mansion dating from 1810 which he had bought in 1941. Donald Davies noticed shawls being woven in the area by a local family called the Farrells and he asked them to make up some of the material in a firmer weave. "When the cloth was perfected," he later explained, "I ordered 5,000 yards." With this lightweight wool, he began to make garments and from the very beginning targeted the American market. "My motivation came from the States. They buttered me up, making me feel like a fine fellow."

On his first trip to New York, he was fortunate to meet Jimmie Booth of the department store Lord & Taylor who took a keen interest in the shirts he was showing. It seems that when she subsequently visited Charleville, she saw one of the Davies sons wearing his school shirt and suggested that his father make the basic garment in a longer style; eventually the Donald Davies shirt dress was created. The man himself told a slightly different version of this story, insisting, "Actually, it was the Paris buyers who said 'make our shirt longer' and it was the American buyers who said, 'okay, kid, belt them.'"

RIGHT **More than two decades after he had first produced the garment forever associated with his name, in 1977 Donald Davies was still winning accolades for his shirt dress. Made from the lightest wool and more often than not belted – as shown here – the item was a staple in every woman's wardrobe and sold around the world. Its simplicity and versatility made it a classic of the era.**

Whatever its origins, the shirt dress was an indisputable success and formed the basis for the company's rapid expansion. The Donald Davies concept became "You can have any length you want, as long as it's a shirt". The Ulster Museum's Elizabeth McCrum feels this garment possessed an inherently American quality in its casual ease. She draws analogies between the Donald Davies shirt dress and the work of Claire McCardle, the New York-based designer who was an early exponent of sportswear. But having only one basic product brought its own challenges, not least the necessity to encourage fresh sales each year. "Everything needs selling," Donald Davies was to explain. "No market keeps expanding unless there is tremendous effort put into the product." This maxim was especially true of his business, because the basic product was so simple and remained largely unchanged for twenty years. Naturally, over successive seasons variations were made to neckline, sleeve styling and length of skirt, but the basic shirt dress stayed consistent, as did its popularity.

There were other elements in the collection offered to the public, long skirts and co-ordinating ruffle-fronted shirts, for example, and the company was conscious of seasonal shifts in fashion. A 1971 photograph of Dublin model Mary Quigley shows her wearing Donald Davies hot pants. Nonetheless, the shirt dress was the core of the business. Donald Davies's wife Mary was responsible for producing new fabric designs each season and these were known for their brilliant jewel colours and arresting patterns, especially bold windowpane checks. In addition to fine woven wools, the company also used light tweeds and linen, the latter described by Donald Davies in 1976 as "smothered in print –

this helps the creases not to show – and it's the coolest cloth in the world, unadulterated linen".

At the very beginning, the Davieses had installed a factory in Charleville's stableyard and as a result, overseas buyers and members of the press frequently visited their home, which became one of the most photographed houses in Ireland. Donald Davies possessed remarkable marketing skills, and he opened up new markets which the great majority of Irish companies had not yet thought of tapping. His son Anthony, who worked in the family business, travelled to Japan long before anyone else gave that country consideration, and as a result there was soon demand for Donald Davies dresses in Tokyo and other major cities. Cecily McMenamin, who worked for the company from 1963 to 1970, remembers just how popular Donald Davies's clothes were. For several years, she was responsible for the company's retail operations in London where there were two shops, on Queen Street and Elizabeth Street. Among the clients were models Jean Shrimpton and Penelope Tree, actresses Liza Minnelli and Catherine Deneuve and fashion photographer David Bailey. In addition, Donald Davies opened outlets in other English towns such as Norwich, Bury St Edmunds and Cambridge.

In April 1968, he opened premises carrying his name on Paris's Avenue Matignon; by this date, he announced, he was exporting eight-five per cent of the clothes he made in four Irish factories. "He had a huge business," Cecily McMenamin recalls. "There must have been over five hundred accounts around the world, and he had agents selling in Britain, the Far East, Australia and North America." Prices were relatively inexpensive, which helps to explain their abiding popularity with customers. Shirts started at five guineas, those with a lace trim at 12 guineas and shirt dresses at 15 guineas. "At the beginning, it was like the nearest thing to Laura Ashley," says Cecily McMenamin, "and very similar in character; everything came from the countryside."

In January 1978, the Davieses sold Charleville, leaving Ireland shortly afterwards, and although the business continued for some time, it eventually folded. Donald Davies's son Anthony had been killed in a car crash some years earlier, and with his death much of the spirit pushing the company forward seems to have disappeared. The shirt dress is still remembered with much affection. Tarlach de Blacam of Inis Meain knitwear says, "On my travels around the world visiting quality stores, I'm always reminded of Donald Davies. People still ask about the product, where is it, because it sold so well. They all seem to have carried it and to miss it now. He had a fantastic name and so it's a pity he disappeared." But perhaps there would not have been a long-term future in any case. "If Donald Davies were working today," argues Elizabeth McCrum, "it might be difficult because he was a one-design person and he'd probably be appealing to an older clientele than the people who now appreciate cutting-edge fashion." The company's success was as much happy coincidence as anything else. "The whole thing grew like Topsy," says Cecily McMenamin. "Donald never had a five-year plan or anything."

Richard Lewis

At the time, this casual approach to business was the norm rather than the exception in the fashion industry. "The sixties were a fun time," remembers designer Richard Lewis. "I wasn't a great businessman – I'm still not – but I'd work hard in spates and then party. There wasn't the same sense of responsibility as there is now." Richard Lewis also recognised right from the start of his career that women were now looking for something other than ladylike suits and coats.

Born in Dublin, he went to the Grafton Academy in 1963 and graduated two years later. "At the time it was the only place to train and I was the only man there, so I probably got a little bit more attention than the others. We had to learn how to sew and make dresses which I hated, but looking back it was a very good training because I understand exactly how a garment goes together and what I can and can't do." Almost immediately after leaving the Academy and aged barely 20, he began selling clothes under his own label. "My mother manufactured school uniforms and nuns' habits and a room beneath her premises became vacant, so I rented it for £2 a week, hired a machinist and basically just started making dresses. I sold to places like Switzer's and Brown Thomas, just two or three pieces at a time. Initially they bought them just for their windows or for shows, not thinking they would sell, and then everyone was quite surprised when they sold. The

Although often compared to Jean Muir, Richard Lewis has acknowledged that during the first decade of his career he was more influenced by Ossie Clark and Barbara Hulanicki of Biba; there are certainly echoes of both in this floral printed corduroy day dress in shades of claret and moss green dating from 1973.

ABOVE The essence of Richard Lewis's style was established very early in his career. This dark brown moss crepe evening dress was made in 1967, and yet it could almost have come from his most recent collection. There is evident a fluidity of movement about the form and an emphasis on femininity, both of which have always been very typical of his style.

LEFT From the moment she began modelling in the late 1970s, Sharon Bacon was associated with designer Richard Lewis. Here she wears a typical example of Lewis's work in his favourite fabric, matt jersey. A navy dress with batwing sleeves, it is edged and belted in a contrasting cranberry colour.

clothes were very trendy at a time when Irish fashion was still back in the fifties. What I was doing was considered very avant garde."

In the *Sunday Press* in May 1970, Terry Keane remarked on the designer's "defiantly individual view of fashion and a readiness to defend it at the slightest provocation with verve, wit and candour". Richard Lewis inevitably seemed different from other designers of the era because his choice of fabrics was novel; a fashion forecast for 1966 in the *Evening Press* picked him out as a name to watch and remarked that he "prefers softer fabrics like printed corduroy, jersey and crepe. His little black dresses in crepe with Op-Art embellishment are a delight". He says that although he did try using tweed at one point in a collection, "it didn't work. It's not my style which is more fluid and not typically Irish at all". During the 1960s, he tended to use quite a lot of printed materials and his style showed certain similarities to that of designer Ossie Clark, then working in London; both men liked to offer women clothes which were soft and tended to caress the body. By the 1970s Richard Lewis had evolved the signature style he has retained ever since. His preference is for solid blocks of colour, especially black, and for fabrics such as silk crepe and jersey; as a result of the latter's preponderance in almost every collection he has produced over the past twenty-five years, he is often called the Irish Jean Muir. In October 1975, Joan Tighe of the *Evening Herald* summarised his look as being based on soft, supple fabrics so that "always gentle, the clothes have pleating and draping and a billowy effect that doesn't add any bulk to the design". "I don't think my style has changed drastically," he confirms. "I don't like masculine or hard-edged clothes on women. I like soft, sexy ones and that has stayed pretty much the same."

In October 1969, Richard Lewis opened his own boutique in a basement at 120 Lower Baggot Street in Dublin where he sold a full range of his own clothes, described by the *Irish Times* at the time as having "great appeal to all girls throughout their twenties". "There was a rash of trendy young boutiques at the time," he now remembers. "I just called mine the Richard Lewis Shop. It had black and white floor tiles and chocolate brown walls and we played Ravi Shankar all the time. I sold minis and little see-through mini-dresses, maxi coats and matching trousers. I bought coatstands and painted them brown and hung all the clothes off them. It wasn't a great commercial success but it was great fun." When the shop closed, he went into partnership with a number of businessmen to produce a relatively inexpensive label called Aquarius, aimed at both the domestic and international markets. Although the company did well for a number of years, it eventually folded.

Since then, Richard Lewis has had a couple of other ventures into ready-to-wear (at one stage in the mid-1990s, he produced a line for the A Wear chain in Ireland) but he is primarily a couturier with a devoted following in Dublin. "We have fashion shows twice a year. The client then makes an appointment, chooses the garment and it's made up for her. There's always at least one fitting and it usually takes about three weeks from start to completion. It's a one-to-one business with everything made for the client." Back in November 1977, when the designer moved into the salon premises on Dublin's South Frederick Street where he has remained ever since, fashion writer Ruth Kelly wrote: "Richard is a dressmaker in the very real sense of the word. He makes the most beautiful and flattering dresses."

Like Thomas Wolfangel, Richard Lewis has now been in business for more than three decades and offers proof that there is still demand in Ireland for couture clothing. But that demand was already shrinking by the end of the 1960s and in the harsh decade about to follow, it would quickly become much smaller.

declining market: 1970–80

In January 1967, the *Irish Independent's* Ita Hynes wrote a feature saluting Ireland's fashion revolution over the previous fifteen years and predicting an even better future for the business. "From a small, not too efficient industry that could not supply the home market, let along export, it has become a high-powered, efficient money-spinner, that can supply markets in every continent." She then went on to imagine still greater success for Irish fashion, "and the sort of growth and development that will see the industry face the invigorating if chilly wind of free trade in five years' time" (when Ireland was to enter the EEC). Regrettably, her forecasts were over-optimistic; even before the decade closed, the 1960s had failed to live up to the promises held out at its start and the 1970s proved to be very tough indeed.

In his book, *Ireland, A Cultural and Social History 1922-1979*, Terence Brown observed that "ostentatious consumption in a society enjoying a rapid rise in its living standards marked the seventies in Ireland as in no other country in modern history." But this improvement in living standards came at a high price; by 1976 inflation was running at an annual rate of 18 per cent. Manufacturing and labour costs both rose sharply, making Irish goods much more expensive and, following admission to the EEC, the country was more vulnerable to cheap imports from abroad. Older businesses could no longer compete in the clothing market, and many of them were forced to close down between the late 1960s and early 1980s.

A report on the state of the country's clothing industry in the *Irish Times* in July 1978 noted that this sector was losing an average 1,000 jobs per year, even though the amount of pay workers could expect to receive – around £35 a week for women – was lower than elsewhere. But, as the article pointed out, "the effects of tariff barriers coming down, the Anglo-Irish Free Trade Agreement and EEC entry – plus the recession – has cut job and wage levels drastically." It quoted a representative from Michael Gall, one of the best-known Irish clothing companies at the time, remarking of the cheap goods brought into the country, "It's our jobs those vans are hitting. They're unloading imported stuff there day and night from Third World countries because the EEC says we have to take it. It's going to send this industry to pieces." In 1958, there were some 22,000 clothing workers in Ireland; twenty years later that figure had fallen to 14,000 and was still dropping. The situation scarcely improved during the 1980s, when net output in the industry declined by 13 per cent and employment by 24 per cent.

Couture market

Couture, which had been primarily responsible for the invention of Irish fashion in the 1950s also began to go into gradual decline from the late 1960s onwards. Elizabeth McCrum observes: "Many designers decided to shut up businesses at the same time and for the same reasons. In the late 1960s something happened which a lot of people never thought would: Paris and couture lost their supremacy. What was new and exciting was coming from youthful designers working with cheap, man-made fabrics. There was a new concept of fashion and a new customer who didn't want something that would last for a long time. She wanted something for £5 that would last a month. It was a given truth at the time that couture was dead – even though eventually it didn't die – and that the cutting-edge of fashion design lay elsewhere." During a three-year period, three major names in the business closed their doors: Irene Gilbert in 1969; Neilli Mulcahy a year later; and Clodagh in 1972. Writing about the disappearance of couture in the *Irish Times* at the end of the 1970s, Patsey Murphy observed that this kind of clothing "after a very successful period in the 'sixties and early 'seventies, can no longer survive without expansion. There simply isn't the money or the market to support it." But even quality manufacturers found survival difficult. In 1972, Jack Clarke closed his Country Wear factory in order to concentrate on the retail market. His two sons later remembered, "he found trying to keep quality and service, with prices continually rising, resulted in a higher selling bracket, which meant less volume and greater difficulties in keeping a factory of over 200 people working for 50 weeks of the year." Some companies survived by adapting to changed circumstances. Avoca Handweavers, for example, which has a history dating back to the 18th century when it produced blankets, was in the earlier part of the century run by three sisters called the Misses Wynne. The company was later sold on and seemed destined for permanent closure when it was bought in 1974 by Donald and Hilary Pratt who found just two weavers still working for the company. Avoca Handweavers is now a substantial family business offering a wide range of clothing for men, women and children and with eight retail outlets in Ireland; the largest, at Kilmacanogue, County Wicklow on eleven acres of gardens, opened in July 1988. "We are by no means an exceptional family," Donald Pratt was quoted as saying at the time, but this was something of an understatement. By constantly examining changes in the market and responding speedily, the company has managed not just to survive but thrive under what others have found impossible circumstances.

Irish fabrics

Aside from manufacturers' inability to compete with cheap imports (an ongoing problem by no means exclusive to Ireland), from the late 1960s onwards there have been other new challenges facing Irish fashion. Not least of these is the unpalatable fact that the basic raw materials used to produce indigenous clothing are no longer as popular as they once were either at home or abroad. An obvious instance of this shift in taste is provided by the history of linen in Ireland. More than any other cloth, linen has enjoyed a close association with the country for hundreds of years. In the late 19th century, some 240,000 acres of land were planted with flax, the plant from which linen is derived. During the early part of the 20th century, linen production and its attendant industries such as shirt-making had been one of the major sources of employment, particularly in Northern Ireland. In 1949 linen accounted for almost 29 per cent of all Northern Irish manufacturing business, but by 1975, that figure stood at a little over five per cent. Similarly, whereas the number of people employed in Northern Ireland's textile industry was almost 58,000 in 1960, by the end of the decade it had fallen to 43,5000.

The problem lay with the basic material; linen requires high maintenance and few consumers had any interest in fabrics needing more than minimal care. Over the past twenty years, linen has come in and out of fashion among designers and this intermittent popularity has helped to sustain a modest industry in Northern Ireland, where just a handful of companies remain in business. In the mid-1980s, for example, Ulster Weavers of Belfast, the only survivor of the old large companies, invested some £2.5 million in a modernisation programme, and other businesses soon did the same. But the combination of seasonal shifts in taste and high production costs means that Irish linen will in future be a luxury item rather than a fashion staple.

Linen at least continues to be produced but demand for other native materials such as silk poplin went into terminal decline. The origins of silk poplin dated from the arrival in Ireland of Huguenot weavers at the end of the 17th century. By using pure silk warp and woollen worsted weft in equal weight proportions, they produced poplin which remained in vogue for dresses until the present century. The last company to manufacture the material, Thomas Elliott & Son, continued in business until 1966 when its Dublin premises were gutted by fire; prior to that date, Irish designers had favoured the fabric, especially for evening wear. But even by the time Elliott's closed, it was becoming clear that poplin would have a very small market in future. In 1974, a newly-formed company in County Cork made efforts to revive the business; a much-publicised dinner was held in Dublin's Tailors' Hall at which dresses designed by a number of Irish designers including Mary O'Donnell, Ib Jorgensen and Thomas Wolfangel were shown. However, silk poplin is a couture fabric and so suffers from limited demand. In addition, the sumptuous, heavy clothing for which it is best suited has fallen from vogue. Indeed, if there is one trend in fashion over the past thirty years which has been to the detriment of Irish cloth producers, it has been the steady and irreversible move towards technologically advanced and lighter fabrics.

Thanks to the introduction of central heating, consumers no longer need to wear clothing primarily for warmth; clothes became lighter (and fewer) as the 20th century progressed. Naturally, this shift in taste affected the country's tweed producers and the best of them discontinued manufacturing heavy cloths in favour of material in lighter weights. One company which recognised in good time that it needed to change in order to meet new market demands was Magee's. Founded in 1866, the Donegal-based business has been owned by the Temple family since 1901 and used to specialise in producing heavy tweeds for businessmen's suiting, which it also manufactured. But by the late 1960s, it became clear that there was no future in such cloth. "We faced a major job to change our image at this time, " Lynn Temple has said. "We tackled the problem with considerable success, although it is a painstakingly slow process to change one's image. We had to make our garments acceptable to today's executives while still giving a degree of durability and good value for money." By the early 1990s, Magee's was producing in the region of 4,000 suits a week, with Germany providing the company's largest market; exports had come to represent 80 per cent of the business.

Lynn Temple explained the decision was taken to focus on the international market, "because, unless we were seen to be a European player, we would almost certainly be regarded as second-rate by our customers. We have invested heavily in market development in Europe, our executives spend a great deal of time abroad and we now have a full-time export sales manager." The investment paid off. In 1999, annual turnover had reached approximately £20 million and close to 600 people were employed between two factories in Ballymena and Donegal. While the old, heavy-weight hand-woven tweeds continue to be manufactured by the company, fresh markets were being wooed in the late 1990s with a John Magee label which used lighter fibres in blends such as linen and silk, as well as pure wool. The younger customer was acknowledged through the introduction of new shapes and colours. Management at Magee's possesses an awareness, not shared by many similar Irish businesses, that fashion must never stop looking toward the future.

Exports

Thanks to companies such as Magee's, and despite the fall in numbers of people employed by manufacturers, the value of Irish exports continued to rise even during some of the worst years of the 1970s and early 1980s. In 1974, exports of clothing were worth £42.9 million; four years later, the figure was £70.5 million. The players who remained in the game were much more aware of its rules and much tougher in their approach. They were often now more keenly aware of the benefits of good design, thanks to advice from bodies such as Coras Tráchtála. This organisation, in conjunction with a number of clothing companies, set up the Irish Fashion Institute in 1974 to inform the industry on future trends in terms of colour, fabric and garment styling. A year later, the annual Coras Tráchtála report could state: "The establishment of the IFI has meant that for the first time the fashion industry has the advantage of full forecasting services related to firms' specific needs." For a time, this certainly seemed to be beneficial. A 1978 report in the *Irish Times* observed that "many more companies are taking advice from consultant designers to bring their styling up to specific export markets and they can now compete with the best in the world." However, in 1980, after just six years in existence, the IFI ceased operations, owing to insufficient support from the very industry it had been created to help.

Flight of young designers

In any case, by the mid-1970s opportunities for designers, consultant or otherwise, were few in the slimmed-down world of Irish fashion. At the same time, colleges were producing more fashion graduates than ever before; it was, after all, precisely during this period that both the National College of Art and Design in Dublin and Limerick School of Art began to offer students courses in this area. Having finished their training, they frequently followed the example of countless young Irish people before them and left the country. Emigration, after seemingly going into retreat in the early 1960s, returned once more and became the scourge of the following two decades; in 1986, for example, it was estimated that as many as 100,000 Irish citizens left their country to look for work elsewhere. They moved abroad because Ireland seemed a drab place offering few opportunities of any kind. "I left Ireland in October 1979 and it was a very different country then to what it is today," Godfrey Deeny says. "Unemployment was at sixteen or seventeen per cent and even though there'd been a bit of a boom in the 1960s, there was a sense that the country was rather underdeveloped. In terms of style, fashion and good living, it was very modest in its aspirations. I remember thinking how poorly people were dressed compared to New York where I went to live for five years. The men at home all seemed to wear really rather bad ill-fitting suits and all the women were in pleated skirts and old blazers. There was no real pizazz or polish about anywhere." This constant departure of young talent was bound to have a detrimental effect on Irish fashion. The industry remained intensely conservative because the more innovative designers went abroad in search of work, and yet conservative clothes were not what the domestic market wanted to buy. Naturally, some Irish designers will always move to other countries. Ireland is too small to provide opportunities for all its design graduates. But staying at home hardly appeared even an option in the 1970s.

Lorcan Mullany

The careers of two Irish designers from the period who found opportunities abroad may be taken as typical of their generation's experience. "The reason I left," explains Lorcan Mullany, "was that there weren't jobs at that time for a designer in Ireland, there wasn't any place to work. You had to leave." Born in Bansha, County Tipperary, he always wanted to be a designer even though his father hoped he would take over the family farm. "I don't remember Ireland as being a fashionable place then, but in a way people always dressed well. My mother certainly dressed well. She had an old-fashioned drapery shop that sold everything from wellingtons to communion suits. I think I got a lot from her, both in a perfectionist way and in a style way; she was very low key and liked good quality and that was a big influence on me."

Although he was making clothes from childhood onwards, Lorcan Mullany spent a year at agricultural college in County Limerick in order to please his father before he was able to go to the Grafton Academy. "It was like a breath of fresh air because this was the first time I was good at something; I was never any good at school. We learnt pattern-cutting mostly which quite baffled me at the start. The girls in the class had worked with patterns before but I'd never seen them and thought, 'is that a sleeve, or what?' Now I'm quite obsessive about patterns. I almost make them, it's still a real thing with me."

Although he was very successful at the Academy, winning a number of student prizes during his two and a half years there, Lorcan Mullany immediately moved to England after graduation. "I left because I knew I wanted to do eveningwear and at the time there wasn't anywhere in Ireland I could go to work. I was always attracted to the bright lights, so it was either London or New York."

In fact, in the mid-1970s he settled in London where, having worked for a year with a theatrical costumier business, he spent time with both Hardy Amies and Bill Gibb. He then moved into mass production with Ronald Joyce, where he became design director and produced a collection under his own name, before finally settling in 1987 with Bellville Sassoon, a long established English house where he is responsible for ready-to-wear. "I've been lucky to find Lorcan," his partner David Sassoon has said. "The new generation is another direction. That's the art of survival – always look forward."

Among the Irish designer's most famous customers at Bellville Sassoon/Lorcan Mullany was the late Diana, Princess of Wales. "I first met her when I was still doing my own collection and was selling at an exhibition in Olympia. She was on a royal walkabout, came onto my stand and ordered a plain black dress. The same day, the Duchess of Kent came and ordered the same dress, so there was a bit of a tussle but you can imagine who I gave the dress to. She was wonderful as a customer; very sweet and grateful, polite and well-mannered. She wasn't really a clotheshorse. She liked clothes but didn't want to spend a whole day over sketches like a lot of people. She was a joy to dress and always looked good in the clothes." Two of the best-known dresses he designed for the Princess of Wales were included in the sale of her clothes in June 1997, two months before her death. One was a knee-length black and white cocktail dress – "actually she saw it in a magazine and just rang up" – and the other a black evening dress with jewelled shoulder-straps.

Lorcan Mullany has been based in London for more than a quarter of a century and it now seems highly unlikely that he will ever move back to Ireland, even though he says he would like to return home and visits the country twice a year to see his sisters. "I think there is a residue of Ireland in me. I only realised recently that everything about me is Irish Catholic. All my values are so typically of that time."

Peter O'Brien

Another exceptionally talented designer who now seems forever lost to Ireland is Dubliner Peter O'Brien. Leaving school in his mid-teens, he spent a number of years working as a window dresser at Best's and then Arnott's department stores before moving to London. "With the arrogance of youth," he remembers, "I thought Dublin dreary and everyone there incredibly plain and wearing hideous shoes and ugly clothes. Fashion for me was anywhere else but Dublin. I loved glamour, artifice and disguise and everyone in Dublin seemed very classic and stuffy." In London, he applied to St Martin's College of Art where he studied fashion for four years, followed by a further year in New York's Parson's College. Like Lorcan Mullany, his primary interest lay in understated but beautiful eveningwear, so in the 1970s he had to look outside Ireland for employment. "When you grow up in a working class neighbourhood like Finglas," he now says, "you feel there are lots of things that don't belong to you like theatres or bookshops or going to college. I never thought they were accessible to me and the only way to break this pattern was to go elsewhere and reinvent myself as a fashion designer."

Peter O'Brien moved to Paris in 1981 and was employed in the workshops of both Dior and Givenchy before being offered a job as assistant to the head designer at the house of Chloe. Here, he eventually became head designer for two seasons in 1986/87 and then, following a few years' freelancing, in July 1990 he was invited to relaunch the Rochas fashion label, which had been in abeyance for forty years. Shortly after this appointment, Peter O'Brien commented "People invariably say, 'my God, an Irish designer, how curious,' as though it's totally impossible that anyone coming from Ireland could be a designer. So I have to start screaming about Sybil Connolly and Irene Gilbert."

Nonetheless, despite this keen awareness of his country's fashion past, he has chosen to settle outside Ireland because at a crucial time in his career, the opportunities were not available at home. "I wanted to design clothes that were very luxurious, very elegant but in a very quiet way," he told the *Irish Times*' Kathryn Hone in 1990, and this he has been able to do in Paris where his work is notable for its spirit of understated richness. There remain influences of Ireland in Peter O'Brien's clothes; in the press information provided at his spring/summer 1998 show for Rochas, there were quotations from Mollie Keane and Oscar Wilde as well as Nancy Mitford and E.F. Benson. "Everyone says my colours are very Irish," he once remarked. "I like sort of half-tones rather than primary colours." And he is not averse to using classic Irish forms such as the Aran sweater, albeit in more luxurious materials than is usually the case, teamed with a full silk crepe or taffeta evening skirt. Peter O'Brien also tends to adopt the low-key approach to dressing which Lorcan Mullany mentioned as being, in his opinion, typically Irish. "I love grey flannel," he declared when he first started to work with Rochas and he regularly uses tweed from Irish manufacturers in his collections. Many of the clothes are nostalgic in character, harking back to the 1920s and 1930s in their combination of technical skill and apparent simplicity.

Although for many years he rarely returned to Ireland, more recently he has been a regular visitor to the country and comments, "When I now see Irish fashion, there is a gentleness and romanticism definitely about the way the women dress. They love chenille and all that textured stuff. It's not aggressive, there are always lots of long skirts, even during periods when they're not in fashion. And I suppose the woman I design for is not in any way aggressive either." While he would like to return to live in Ireland, after eighteen years working in Paris this now seems an unlikely scenario. "If I did a collection at home, I'm not sure there'd be enough business. I'd probably have to bring it to London or Paris. The whole system I know is here in France. One of the great advantages of Paris is the quality of workmanship you can get, especially if you love technique and the way clothes are made. The French make wonderfully luxurious clothes and they produce everything here. If you're doing a fitting and you want orange chiffon, you just make a few phone calls and forty-five shades of orange are available to you."

Ever since the 1970s, large numbers of Irish designers have left their own country to work abroad. Many of them today do not manufacture under their own names but are employed by clothing companies in London, Paris, Milan and New York. Jacqueline Quinn, yet another former student of the Grafton Academy, has been living and working in Manhattan since the mid-1990s. Before then, she had taken jobs with a number of Irish businesses. "I was frustrated with the lack of money companies at home paid to designers" is her explanation for moving across the Atlantic. In New York, she is responsible for import designs at John Roberts, a label with an annual turnover in the region of $100 million. But in 1999, she produced a collection under her own name and has hopes that this might be carried by retailers in Ireland.

A common characteristic among Irish designers working abroad – and indeed among Irish emigrants in general – is a desire, if not to return home, at least to see what they produce on sale in Ireland. From the early 1970s onwards, to leave their own country in search of work elsewhere became a norm among graduates in every discipline, including fashion. Remembering when she left university in the early 1980s, Paula Reed says, "Unfortunately at the time, my contemporaries were all having to look for jobs out of the country. It was a very different economic prospect to try and start a career in Ireland then. Everyone at that date moved away, we were scattered all over." It was only at the very end of the century that economic circumstances had improved sufficiently to suggest Ireland could once more support a substantial indigenous fashion industry. But by then, more than one generation of talent had been lost to the country. The few designers who remained enjoyed a relatively uncrowded market and, as the 1970s progressed, this situation was to prove both an asset and a disadvantage.

RIGHT **During the years when Peter Fitzsimons worked for Michael Jacobs, his clothes were always identifiable by their sense of dash and sparkle. That is certainly the case with this pair of trouser suits and their accompanying strapless tops dating from the late 1970s, when the disco craze was at its height.**

Although Irish fashion had to face substantial challenges during the 1970s, a number of developments in the same period would be of long-term benefit. One of these was the emergence of new publications in which local talent was promoted. Now an established presence among Irish magazines, *Image* made its debut in October 1975 with a cover price of just 25 pence. A characteristic trait from the very first issue was the assumption that Irish fashion belonged in an international context. In *Image's* pages, therefore, clothes from Ireland would be shown alongside those from other countries. Similarly, while the model on the cover might be Irish, she could well be dressed in French or English fashion. *Image* always encouraged Irish design, but never in isolation.

Four years later, in October 1979, *I.T.* appeared for the first time. This was editor Noelle Campbell Sharp's makeover of a long-established but uninspiring title, the *Irish Tatler and Sketch*. In its reincarnation as *I.T.*, the magazine was youthful, vibrant and self-confident in its advocacy of Irish fashion. In every issue, at least one of the country's designers was given a four- or six-page spread, as often photographed (by the editor's husband Neil Campbell Sharp) in Italy or the South of France as Ireland. Like the work in *Image*, these shoots had the effect of placing Irish fashion alongside its equivalents elsewhere. *I.T.* was particularly keen to emphasise that not only were the clothes produced in Ireland of equal standard to those found elsewhere, but they were also usually cheaper. In April 1980, for example, the editorial accompanying a fashion shoot noted that "several Irish manufacturers, like Patrick Howard, are gaining increasing respect today from Irish fashion-conscious women who now realise they are obtaining better quality and the very latest fashion design for a good deal less than their fashion-conscious counterparts can buy abroad." "I think Noelle led the way in the fashion promotion business," says clothing manufacturer Michael Jacobs. "She got the whole of the Irish fashion industry together in one magazine and it was very well done. In terms of business, it paid off to do promotions with *I.T.* because the public took what was shown seriously."

A key feature of the 1970s, therefore, was Irish fashion's acknowledgement of shifting global trends. One reason for this was the declining interest in the country's indigenous materials. These had helped to define the character of clothes design in Ireland during earlier decades but were now out of favour both at home and abroad. "There was a shift around 1970," according to Elizabeth McCrum. "While one group of designers continued working in a recognisably Irish way, another group of mostly male designers were working in an international mode. They might have used Irish fabrics and enjoyed playing with them but you couldn't define their clothes as Irish like you could in the 1950s and 1960s." "Our fashion was a very fragile little flower in the seventies," comments journalist Terry Keane. "It was an uphill struggle because nobody wanted tweed and linen anymore and people abroad couldn't see us as a fashion force. And the Irish themselves often didn't wear Irish design." This was why the promotion of local designers by magazines such as *I.T.* and *Image* was to be so important.

Muriel Kerr

Lighter fabrics and more casual clothing demanded a different approach to fashion from that taken by the previous generation of Irish clothing manufacturers and designers. It was a retailer who, instead of bemoaning the changes taking place, recognised what exciting opportunities this presented to the domestic market. Originally from Northern Ireland, Muriel Kerr opened her first Mirror, Mirror outlet on Dublin's Nassau Street in 1974; by the time the business went into liquidation a decade later, the company had sixteen branches around the country employing 300 staff. Mirror, Mirror – like the new Irish fashion magazines – was successful because it realised consumers wanted clothing with an international flavour at affordable prices. An assessment of the business in the *Irish Times* in April 1981 noted that before the arrival of Mirror, Mirror the Irish fashion scene had offered a "bleak picture" and a "woefully limited look" to young women who, like Muriel Kerr's own daughter, "saved all their pennies and hightailed it to London to do all their shopping…obviously Dublin was wide open for people with fashion sense, enterprise and capital." Regrettably, the company grew too big too fast and therein lay the origins of its eventual collapse in the summer of 1984, when debts of over £1 million led to inevitable closure. But in the late 1970s and early 1980s, Mirror, Mirror was like a three-dimensional version of

Coats have always been one of the great strengths of Irish designer manufacturers. This wrapover model from autumn/winter 1981 is by Michael Jacobs, who continues to work in clothing but now concentrates on making corporate wear in which his tailoring skills can be put to good use.

Image's fashion pages; it mixed international labels with Irish ones and made no discrimination between the two. At the time, this was precisely what the industry required – a tough lesson in survival among global competitors. The outcome was a new attitude to fashion in Ireland with dependence on winsome tradition being jettisoned in favour of international modernism.

Peter Fitzsimons

In the mass market, the designer who best represented this approach was Peter Fitzsimons. A Dubliner whose family had worked in the men's tailoring trade for generations, he never had a business under his own name but still achieved widespread recognition thanks to the consistently high quality of the work he produced. Although only 41 when he died in March 1989, Peter Fitzsimons had had a long career because he started so young, leaving school at the age of 14. In 1974, he went to work as designer for Michael Jacobs, who had been running his own business for five years. It was an association that was to prove highly advantageous to both parties. "Peter was very astute," Michael Jacobs remembers. "He knew the Irish market and what was coming on. He had a really sophisticated marketing skill and kept constant contacts with the people who were buying for stores. And he was very good at promotion among the press." That press included Terry Keane who says she saw Peter Fitzsimons's work at the first fashion show he held for the Michael Jacobs label in Sachs Hotel, Dublin. "I wasn't expecting anything but if there is any such thing as an overnight success, it was Peter after that show. I went straight to see him and said I was going to give him a page the following week. He soon made the company into a household name."

For Terry Keane, as for everyone else at the time, Peter Fitzsimons's strength lay in his ability to interpret contemporary trends for the Irish market without compromise. The 1970s was the decade in which trouser suits for women came into favour and he excelled at well-cut (and well-priced) tailoring. "Peter had a brilliant feel for fabrics and brought Irish fashion away from the tweedy, soft look to a more hard-edged, clean silhouette," Terry Keane confirms. "Plus, he was able to translate very quickly the Paris

According to *Image* magazine in April 1980, Michael Jacobs's blazers "are right in line with the current word from Paris and, teamed with simple skirts, make for that neat sporty look that everyone will be wearing this spring and summer."

runways. You could buy from him a beautifully-cut coat or suit in a superb fabric at a reasonable price. He wouldn't have claimed to be a great innovator – there are never very many of them – but he was a superb translator of what was happening." The same point was made in an *Irish Times* review in February 1978 of his spring/summer collection which said, "he has scooped up and interpreted all the latest ideas". Peter Fitzsimons acknowledged this himself in a feature in the January 1980 issue of *I.T.*, remarking that designers "must know what goes on at grass-roots level. I make a regular tour of all the leading fashion shops in Dublin every week so I can quickly ascertain what Irish women want to wear." By this date, he had left Michael Jacobs and gone to work with another company, Peerless Fashions, where he designed a label called Private Collection.

Noelle Campbell Sharp remembers, "Peter was the first person really interested to find out what was going on in Paris and other cities. I once brought back an Yves Saint Laurent suit for him to take apart so that he could study how it was done; he put it back together afterwards and returned it to me." There was nothing specifically Irish in either cut or fabric about Peter Fitzsimons's work. Instead, it was a confident résumé of contemporary international trends for the local market. There seemed to be no technical detail he was not capable of mastering and his clothes were full of clever cutting, pleating and draping. Best of all, they were for sale at an affordable price; £75 for a wool flannel skirt suit in 1980 and £59.95 for a bouclé coat. The combination of excellent workmanship and keen pricing was what won him new admirers. "For those of us who'd usually be working with couturiers," says former model Marguerite MacCurtin, "to find someone producing really excellent clothing with innovative design was a rare phenomenon. Peter's tailoring was extraordinarily good and he certainly had the look of the moment."

The most devoted of his customers was Miranda, Countess of Iveagh . "I remember finding something of his in Dublin," she says, "and then trying to find out who and where he was and that ultimately led me to Michael Jacobs." For Miranda Iveagh, Peter Fitzsimons's style "was slightly aping a men's tailor but he managed to use the right materials so that it always hung beautifully on the female form. Peter had the ability to use extraordinarily fine

Among Peter Fitzsimons's most loyal clients was Miranda, Countess of Iveagh who remembers the designer's style as "slightly aping a men's tailor but he managed to use the right materials so that it always hung beautifully on the female form". Here she is wearing a suit in white – his favourite colour – for the official launch of the vessel *Miranda Guinness* in December 1976.

Peter Fitzsimons's interest in new fabrics led him to take risks, as with this three-piece trouser suit in fake leather. The designer combined a keen eye for upcoming trends with an awareness of his customers' budgetary limitations.

materials but to me his cutting process was his great strength." She wore his clothes constantly and was often photographed in pieces such as a white Peter Fitzsimons suit, much admired in December 1976 when she officially launched the *Miranda Guinness*, a bulk liquid carrier vessel in Dublin port. Sometimes she bought items from his ready-to-wear collection but on occasions he would make a suit or coat specially for her. "We worked terribly well together because he was very kind and gave a lot of attention to the kind of event I'd be attending."

Because she was so well-known, Miranda Iveagh did much to promote Peter Fitzsimons's career. Interviewed by the *Irish Times* in January 1979 after she had been chosen as one of the world's Best-Dressed Women, she announced, "Peter is half a season ahead of everyone." In another interview, she explained that the designer was "aware of every trend and can foretell when it will last. But most of all, it's his enormous concern for detail – satin pipings, the right buttons even – that keeps your interest in fashion as well as just in clothes." In October 1978, Miranda Iveagh took American fashion publicist Eleanor Lambert to meet Peter Fitzsimons who told her, " I design for the world I live in, and that is not a world of erratic changes." Could he, therefore, have survived into another era? According to Terry Keane, "Peter was sufficiently talented that he would have adapted to anything. He could have done a softer silhouette if he were asked to do so." Michael Jacobs, on the other hand, argues that Peter Fitzsimons "never got to grips with casual clothing. The market has changed so dramatically that the tailored product is just no longer wanted; we're still producing it because we're good tailors, but we've moved into corporate wear."

In the late 1970s/early 1980s, Peter Fitzsimons was just one of a number of designers who were catering for women's new-found appetite for trousers and suits. The man with whom he began his career, Michael Jacobs, was another. In the April 1980 issue of *Image*, for example, a feature on Jacobs's clothes observed, "his flair for well-cut suits and dresses sets him ahead of most of his competitors…His blazers are right in line with the current word from Paris and, teamed with simple skirts, make for that neat sporty look that everyone will be wearing this spring and summer." A year later, in May 1981, *I.T.* carried a large spread on another important Irish clothes manufacturer of the time, Michael Gall, whose clothes were then being stocked by the Mirror, Mirror chain. After commenting on the quality of the garments, the editorial added, "what's more, the prices beat anything imported in the same quality".

Patrick Howard

However, the Irish designer who best demonstrated keen awareness of the domestic market's interest in well-produced and reasonably priced clothing, in touch with what was happening elsewhere, was Patrick Howard. "There was a moment in the seventies when every model wore Patrick Howard trousers," Marguerite MacCurtin says. "I remember there was a fashion show for Vard furs and we'd been asked to wear simple black dresses underneath the coats; none of us owned one, but we all had about six pairs of Patrick's trousers." Although he established his reputation with this one item of clothing, there was much more to the Howard repertoire than a pair of trousers, no matter how well-cut. Born in 1949 into a farming family in Ballyvaughan, Co Clare, he says he always knew he wanted to work as a designer. "I suppose I had a natural flair and I only ever wanted to be involved in the fashion business." After leaving school, he moved to Dublin and attended the Grafton Academy of Dress Design for two years. "At the time, the Academy was the only place to go. It was predominantly female then, there was myself and maybe two other

Journalist Terry Keane says that Peter Fitzsimons "had a brilliant feel for fabrics and brought Irish fashion away from the tweedy, soft look to a more hard-edged, clean silhouette." That is certainly true of this Fitzsimons trouser suit in buttermilk corduroy, dating from the mid-1970s.

guys. You'd start in the morning making patterns and probably spent weeks doing just that. Then you went on to garment construction and sewing." Like others of his generation who made their reputation through excellent tailoring, Patrick Howard appreciates the sound training he received while a student. "To be a good designer, it's very important to be good technically," he explains. "By that, I mean being good at pattern-making. If a garment doesn't have a good pattern, it won't fit as well as it should. I think there's a strong inherited tradition in Ireland to produce good pattern-makers like Paul Costelloe, Michael Mortell, Peter Fitzsimons and myself, if I may say so. We made fine patterns for clothes that fitted people very well."

Almost immediately after leaving the Grafton Academy in 1970, Patrick Howard went into business for himself, taking premises on South Frederick Street in Dublin where, with just a handful of staff, he started to produce the trousers for which he initially became renowned. "It was only in the early seventies that women really began to wear trousers all the time," explains Terry Keane. "Yves Saint Laurent produced the most wonderful trouser suits then but not many people could afford them. Patrick was the first person in Ireland to make trousers that looked good; he stopped us all looking a fright. Everyone rushed to his place on South Frederick Street to buy them from him." "I remember there was such a demand for my trousers that I could sell as many as we made," Patrick Howard now says. "It all seemed quite easy because there wasn't much competition out there, there were far fewer of us around and you didn't have the big machines like Dunnes Stores producing wonderful clothes and selling them very well."

Patrick Howard is the perfect example of a designer being in the right place at the right time. Having established himself with trousers, he moved on to produce collections of other tailored items such as suits and coats which were just as popular with consumers. By the end of the seventies, it seemed as though the height of every Irish woman's ambition was to be dressed by Patrick Howard. "He was phenomenally successful," Terry Keane confirms, "but perhaps it all came too easily to him." Similarly, Marguerite MacCurtin remembers "this was the time when trouser suits were the only thing and Patrick's were really beautifully cut and made, so everybody bought them." Like Peter Fitzsimons, the designer was

RIGHT **In the late 1970s and early 1980s, almost every fashionable woman in Ireland owned or was planning to buy one of Patrick Howard's suits. This is a typical example of his work, from 1980, in a fine Irish herringbone tweed. These clothes were ideal for the large number of women who were entering the jobs market and were looking for designs simultaneously practical and stylish.**

Jean O'Reilly was the face of the late 1970s and of designer Patrick Howard in the new fashion magazines such as *I.T.* and *Image*. Here she wears one of his more flamboyant suits from 1978, a boldly-patterned wool skirt and jacket worn with a lace-trimmed black chemise top and gold lamé cummerbund.

an exceptionally good self-publicist and this undoubtedly helped sales. "In the early seventies," he explains, "I devoted a lot of time to the press and talking to journalists. Noelle Campbell Sharp did a lot for me; we'd go away on shoots together at home and abroad and that certainly helped my business in no small way." Early editions of *I.T.* regularly carried pages of Patrick Howard clothing. The very first issue included a shoot of his work featuring the model of the moment, Jean O'Reilly, photographed in St Moritz; a year later in October 1980, the same model wearing clothes by the same designer appeared in *I.T.*'s pages after a shoot in Rome. "These shoots didn't come cheap – they probably cost a few thousand pounds each – but I felt it was worth it," Patrick Howard comments. "The money for them came out of the publicity budget and it was my way of marketing myself at the time."

Patrick Howard's strengths lay in his well-honed tailoring skills and his acute knowledge of the marketplace. He would not describe himself as a major innovator. "One was always dictated to by international looks from London and Paris," he says. "You worked your way around those styles and came up with something that was very commercial. I was always very commercial in my designs. I wanted to sell what I made, so I didn't make much avant-garde stuff. You might do some pieces just for the ramp but those seldom sold in any great quantity." What did sell in large amounts were his suits and coats, not least because they were affordable. His spring/summer range for 1980, for example, included wool jackets for £50 and full, gathered wool plaid skirts for £45. Around this time, he opened premises on Dublin's Dawson Street, his flagship store, but he also had a number of other outlets and a large concessionary area in Switzer's department store.

At its height, his business had an annual turnover in the region of £1 million, a remarkable figure during a period when many other Irish clothing businesses were finding survival difficult. He had a particular fondness for tweeds in strong colours and bold checks. "The fabrics I used at the time were mostly handwoven tweeds and some worsteds and gabardine. I dealt with some of the top mills in the west of Ireland. Connemara Fabrics were a favourite of mine because they were probably the most switched-on, always in tune with the fashion colours for the season and they had the international look which a lot of people in Ireland didn't have."

That international look was what Irish consumers wanted in the 1970s and eighties; they had no interest in anything too overtly local in origin. "Success is giving people what they want," announced the *Irish Times* in April 1977. "Patrick Howard must ask himself each season some basic questions and so far he has come up with the right answers." But in the mid-1990s, he decided to leave the fashion business and become an antique dealer instead. His enthusiasm for clothes, he says, has gone and rather than remain associated with an industry in which he was once a leader, he felt the best choice was to leave it behind.

Paul Costelloe

If Patrick Howard and Peter Fitzsimons have left the scene, other fashion names from the 1970s are still to be found, not least Paul Costelloe who first began trading under his own name at the end of the decade. Before then, he had spent more than ten years gaining experience in the key fashion capitals of the world. Born in Dublin in 1946, he had early understanding of the Irish clothing industry since his father was managing director of a company called Valstar, which produced rainwear. However, he also credits his American mother with inspiring an interest in fashion and it is certainly true that his work has always shown a certain transatlantic character, with its emphasis on casual ease. When he established his business in 1979, he says, "I wanted to bring the American philosophy of casual rather than rigid tailoring to the industry." He describes his ideal client as an American woman from the mid-west, "someone who's well-mannered and just looks cool the whole time. The model Lauren Hutton, even though she's now in her fifties, would be a very typical Paul Costelloe type of person; you never see her over-dressed, she looks confident and comfortable." As a designer, he could be considered the Irish equivalent of Ralph Lauren, projecting an image of understated elegance with clothes which tend not to call attention to themselves. "If anyone thinks buying something from me is going to make her look wonderful, no, that's not the case," Paul Costelloe insists. "You have to be clear, confident and comfortable to wear my clothes. I love independent women and again that would come from my American mother."

Paul Costelloe was one of many Irish designers who received their initial training at the Grafton Academy of Dress Design. Part of the students' work was participation in an annual fashion show, and here a very young Costelloe can be seen on stage with one of his designs from 1966, when he was a prize-winner at the Academy.

Paul Costelloe tends to be at his best when most relaxed, as here in a cardigan and pair of trousers dating from 1984. Items such as these drew him to the attention of the late Diana, Princess of Wales, whom he met at around this time.

It was only after leaving school that he decided to work in fashion and so went to the Grafton Academy. "I suppose I liked women and having a father in the clothing industry, it seemed natural that I should get involved, so I was at the Academy for a year and then at the age of nineteen I went to Paris." Here he spent three years, working for much of the time with couturier Jacques Esterel. In 1968 he was invited to join Marks & Spencer, first in its London headquarters and later in Milan. This was followed by a period with a number of different employers in New York. "Working in America as a designer is all about merchandising," he says. "It's very much more commercial than in Europe. The first man I worked for in New York was not very patient with me, he thought I was too creative." As Paul Costelloe's career has shown, commerce and creativity need not be in opposition to one another. By the late 1970s, he felt he had sufficient experience of both to come back home. "I saw Perry Ellis, who was a very successful designer at the time, using heavy Irish tweeds, linen and knitwear and thought I could do that. So I returned to Ireland and looked for a company to back me. Eventually I found one with Strelitz in County Tyrone, with a good tailoring background and an interest in the export market."

From the very beginning, Paul Costelloe focused not only on the domestic but also the overseas markets. Today, Ireland accounts for in the region of ten per cent of his business, with British stores taking seventy per cent of what he produces. His lifelong links with the United States mean he is particularly keen to establish a closer association with the American market. "Hopefully, we'll have the finance soon to have a presence in New York with a shop, which is one of my ambitions." He has found that using Irish fabrics and having an Irish identity has helped him when exporting his work. "The Irish image for selling in the global market is very sympathetic. It's definitely a plus, but at the end of the day, it's the product that matters and how it's displayed." From the first collections, he has used linen for his spring/summer ranges – "it was one of my main reasons for coming back to Ireland" – but he also tries to include lightweight tweeds whenever possible. "I'm not loyal to Irish materials but I do like working with our mills. I do think the colours I like are Irish; they're not too bold because those don't suit Irishwomen unless they're very beautiful and very young.

I suppose it's my conservative Catholic upbringing which says 'Don't stand out, Mary'. So I take colours which are softer, more subtle, I prefer to use touch to be more effective."

As with other Irish designers who came to prominence in the seventies, Paul Costelloe's greatest strength lies in his tailoring. It was this quality which brought him to the attention of the late Diana, Princess of Wales for whom he made clothes over a number of years in the 1980s. He first met the Princess in 1985 when he was invited to bring a selection of his work to Kensington Palace. "She was very clear about what she wanted, the protocol for different occasions. She was a perfect size 10, maybe the sleeves had to be made a little bit longer and the skirts because she was quite tall. She was always great fun and would even carry the garments back down the stairs and put them into the car, which is more than a lot of my customers would do." Since tailored suiting remained important in women's fashion during the 1980s, this was a very good decade for the designer who says that he has subsequently had to adapt his approach. "My style has changed over a twenty-year period from being heavily tailored and structured to a softness which is still tailored but in a way possibly younger than it used to be. It's got a broader customer base; today somebody 24 and somebody 44 can wear the same outfit. My style now is less harsh, less aggressive and as I'm getting older I'm mellowing."

As his approach to fashion has changed, so too have the circumstances in which Paul Costelloe works. In September 1997, he sold his business for £1.25 million to a British company, Silk Industries, continuing to work as designer under a licensing arrangement which requires him to base his operations in England. He has also been responsible for designing homeware ranges for a number of companies in this field, signing an agreement in December 1998 with china company Wedgwood to develop a line of tableware. Paul Costelloe's awareness of the global market and its potential has been greater than that of most other Irish designers. He has, for example, had his own shop on London's Brompton Road for a number of years and would argue that trying to maintain a strictly national fashion industry is no longer possible. "We have to be aware of all markets now," he says. It was an awareness that Irish designers in the 1980s would have to acquire if they wished to achieve success.

More than any other Irish designer, Paul Costelloe has an American sensibility in his love of casual sportswear. These clothes from his 1982 spring/summer collection include a cotton cable-knit sweater and, beneath it, a tie-neck shirt in one of the designer's favourite fabrics, linen.

7. fighting back: 1980–90

If fashion in Ireland during the 1980s began to show a healthy development, this growth was not necessarily mirrored by the state of the country's economy. For much of the decade, the problems of unemployment, emigration and inflation which had already been evident in the 1970s continued to provide an unhappy presence in Ireland. Naturally, they had an effect on the clothing industry where the number of workers continued to drop; by 1988, the figure had fallen to 11,500. A report produced for the Irish Apparel Industries Federation that same year noted that there were now some 400 clothing companies in the country, but that less than half of these employed more than 100 people. The biggest concentration of such businesses was in the Dublin area - fifty per cent - with Donegal then accounting for a further fifteen per cent.

Many designers continued to face difficulties during the 1980s; a report in the *Irish Times* in March 1988 observed "Our leading designers are struggling hard" before going on to list the number of well-known names who, for financial reasons, would not be staging shows that season. "Irish designers are resourceful and imaginative and they make very good clothes," the piece concluded. "What they need is a loyal public to back them up. Otherwise we will lose a few more every year." Two months earlier, the *Irish Independent* had reported that Irish retailers were also facing difficulties with the country's leading department store, Brown Thomas, announcing weekly losses of £40,000 and another store, Arnott's, looking for 70 redundancies among its 920-strong workforce.

Even while these warnings of imminent doom were being issued, however, exports of Irish clothes had steadily risen. Whereas forty-nine per cent of all garments produced in the Republic were exported in 1980, by 1987 the percentage had increased to almost fifty-six. Coras Tráchtála continued to assist Irish clothing companies wanting to sell overseas, but there were a number of other initiatives as well. In 1982, for example, the Irish Knitwear Exporters' Guild was formed to promote and sell quality knitwear to both the domestic and overseas markets. A decade after its establishment, the guild had twenty-one members and was contributing substantially to the £30 million annual sales of Irish knitwear. In addition, an organisation formed by a group of designers and manufacturers in the 1970s, Irish Fashion

International, began to make an impact on the American market through twice-yearly attendance at trade shows in New York, Chicago and San Francisco.

In Ireland itself, a greater effort was being made to attract overseas buyers, thanks to bodies such as the Irish Fashion Group, formed in 1979 by nineteen manufacturers and backed by the Irish Goods Council. The group held an annual fair in Dublin and by February 1989, ten years after its foundation, its members could collectively expect orders from overseas buyers in the region of £4 million. It later amalgamated with the twice-yearly Futura Fair, a 1970s successor to the Irish Export Fashion Fair, and, like that event, designed to attract large numbers of overseas visitors. Among Futura's own efforts to increase interest in fashion at home was the announcement every autumn of the country's best-dressed woman and man, chosen by a committee representing Ireland's clothes designers and manufacturers. The winners in its first year, 1981, were Miranda, Countess of Iveagh and Baron Brian de Breffny.

Irish Fashion Week

Another much-publicised innovation from the same period was the launch of an Irish Fashion Week in August 1982. Designers from the same country all opting to show their new collections within a short period of time can scarcely be classified as a radical new trend; to facilitate visiting American journalists and buyers, something similar to (but less formally structured than) Irish Fashion Week had already existed in Dublin during the 1950s, but it fell into abeyance once that market became less important. The Irish Fashion Week emerged when seven of the best-known names in the industry - Ib Jorgensen, Paul Costelloe, Henry White, Thomas Wolfangel, Michael Mortell, Richard Lewis and John Rocha, with his then wife Eily Doolin – formed an Irish Designers' Association and, with assistance from the International Wool Secretariat, agreed to present their seasonal collections within the same week.

As the list of members indicates, the association included both couturiers and designers of ready-to-wear clothing; as the *Irish Times* asked afterwards, "Do we have something here that could be called a 'look?' Is it a cohesive picture, or is it just a lot of good

Ritzy, opened in August 1979 by Quin and Donnelly, was notable for its relaxed, casual clothing which reflected trends in London. The two designers travelled to India in search of interesting fabrics, such as the ribbed cotton used here, from 1983. They would buy bales of such material and have it dyed into a wide range of brilliant colours for their clothes.

fragments that won't stand up for long?" These rhetorical questions were probably best left unanswered and the newspaper's report settled for describing the week as "a short, sharp shock of fashion" while the *Sunday Independent* summarised the occasion as "a resounding success". Although Irish Fashion Week continued for a number of years, much praised, it did not even manage to last until the end of the decade, primarily because not all designers could continue to invest in underwriting expensive shows. Without enough participants, the week could not hope to survive.

Irish Design Centre

But another initiative of the 1980s has continued to thrive. In June 1984, the Irish Design Centre opened for business in a building on Dublin's St Stephen's Green. Backed once again by the International Wool Secretariat as well as Coras Tráchtála, twenty young designers were provided with their own small retail outlets for a weekly rental of £60 each. The great merit of the centre, which later moved into the Powerscourt Townhouse Centre, was that it encouraged youthful talent to remain in Ireland and not presume that the only future lay with companies abroad. Instead, there was now the possibility that a small, burgeoning fashion label could have its own presence in Dublin and that fashion-conscious Irish consumers could buy contemporary domestic clothing at a reasonable price. By the time the Design Centre celebrated its tenth anniversary in 1994, it had grown to play host to 25 designers, and enjoyed an annual turnover in the region of £1 million. Among the better-known names who began their careers there are Lainey Keogh and Louise Kennedy.

Ritzy

It would be wrong to suggest that before the arrival of the Irish Design Centre, no young designers had been brave enough to establish their own businesses. However, the economic conditions of Ireland at the time were not encouraging and most fashion graduates understandably chose to look for secure jobs outside the country. Unusually, Carolyn Donnelly and Liz Quin instead opted to stay at home and start their own label and shop, both of which they

By the mid-1980s Quin and Donnelly were making up garments in leather. This two-piece is typical of the time, not just in its exceptionally wide shoulders but also in its awareness of the Japanese designers then making an impact internationally, using details such as the high-buttoning collar and the draping lines of the skirt onto which a large patch pocket has been added at the knee.

Carolyn Donnelly (left) and Liz Quin first met as students at the Grafton Academy of Dress Design in the mid-1970s, and by August 1979 had set up business together. They are exceptional in Ireland, where designers working in pairs are uncommon. Even more unusually, after more than twenty years they continue to enjoy their professional relationship.

called Ritzy. The two women met when they were students at the Grafton Academy, and they opened their business on Dublin's Trinity Street in August 1979. "Are you happy with the mass-produced clothes from the average boutique or fashion department?" their original press release enquired. "Do you enjoy paying ridiculous sums for the toned-down versions of last year's look that our established middle-aged designers produce?" Most young Irish consumers at the time would have answered no to these questions.

"In the early 1980s, Irish fashion was not an inspiring item and did almost nothing for me as a twenty-something," comments Paula Reed. "The people who were successfully making clothes were aimed at my mother's generation. There wasn't a young commercial fashion scene, although there were fantastic people at NCAD and in Trinity who'd make you things; we used to customise stuff that we'd found in second-hand shops. But there weren't any figureheads in Ireland then and we looked to London the entire time because it was trendier." Focusing on this youthful market, Ritzy produced affordable, fashionable young clothing such as baggy tartan trousers, quilted brocade Chinese jackets and double-breasted shift dresses in sherbet colours. There was plenty of demand for what the company produced. "Economically, it was much easier to survive in those days," the two later explained. "We'd give a piece of Irish tweed to people in India and have it woven in cotton."

During the first half of the 1980s, Ritzy thrived and had to move to bigger premises in Clarendon Street. But eventually it fell victim to the same problems which tend to afflict so many fashion businesses; despite having impressive support from Irish, American and British retailers, "We couldn't get financial backing, the rent tripled on the shop, we had orders for what we were doing but not the experience of production set-up to meet them." Eventually Ritzy closed down, but at the end of the 1980s, the pair were given a new contract to design ranges of clothing for the A Wear chain and this they have continued to do ever since under the Quin & Donnelly label.

Fashion Oscars

There were a number of reasons why new ventures like Ritzy or the Irish Design Centre could expect to enjoy good health in the 1980s. Not least among these was a simple matter of demographics; by the start of the decade, more than fifty per cent of the Republic's population was under the age of thirty. This was a generation with a keen interest in the kind of contemporary designs Irish clothing companies had perforce learnt to produce during the 1970s. Couture business may have shrunk but the demand for ready-to-wear grew proportionately. So too did domestic interest in Irish fashion, thanks to the work of publications such as *Image* and *I.T.*, as well as the principal national newspapers. Designers undertook some self-promotion in May

By the early 1990s, Quin and Donnelly had become firmly established as part of the A Wear group, for which they designed this chalk-stripe button-through dress and white cotton blouse in 1993. Their ever-youthful joie-de-vivre is seen in the deep cuffs on the shirt, which also has a band of ruching on the sleeves.

1988 with the debut of a new award scheme, the Satzenbrau Fashion Oscars. Nominees had to be based in Ireland (which automatically and regrettably excluded the many Irish designers working successfully overseas) and to have produced a distinctive performance within and contribution to the country's fashion industry.

The first ceremony included a special presentation to Sybil Connolly "for her outstanding contribution to Irish fashion" while winners included Richard Lewis as Best Designer. The following year that title went to Mariad Whisker, and the Satzenbrau Fashion Oscars seemed set for a long and healthy future. In fact, like so many other such schemes, this one did not even see its tenth birthday, perhaps because the pool of talent from which to draw was so relatively small and the same names began to crop up rather too often. But the Oscars are important because they suggest Irish fashion had regained its self-confidence and sense of worth, qualities all but lost during the previous fifteen years of recession and retrenchment.

Late, Late Fashion Awards

However, the biggest boost to the industry during this period was the inauguration of the Late, Late Fashion Awards, shown on Ireland's most popular television show every October from 1982 onwards. The awards, which later became biennial, reached a bigger audience than any other promotion of Irish fashion had yet managed to achieve and made this area of creativity more accessible to the mass market than before. It also made household names out of Irish designers, not least Michael Mortell who, from the Late, Late Awards' 1982 debut, won the title of Designer of the Year three times in succession.

Michael Mortell

For much of the 1980s, Mortell was Ireland's best-known and most admired fashion designer, accolades not carried lightly by this most self-effacing of men. Early reports often comment on the contrast between his appearance and manner and the world in which he had chosen to work. "Somehow, one never expects to find a big,

With his stocky frame and unruly mop of curls, Michael Mortell bears no resemblance whatever to the stereotypical image of a fashion designer. Originally, he studied fine art but while still a student in Cork he changed his career plans after winning a fashion scholarship to Manchester College of Art.

brawny rugby player at the head of a successful fashion operation," exclaimed the *Irish Independent* in 1979 while a year later, the *Irish Press* was remarking that, while the fashion world "often seems to be full of phonies", Michael Mortell was most certainly not one of them.

The explanation for this want of phoniness may lie in the designer's background and training. Born in 1950 in Mallow, County Cork, he is the youngest of ten children raised over the family's fish and poultry shop. At first he had no intention of becoming a designer, although he did want to be an artist and attended the Crawford School of Art in Cork city. From there he won a scholarship to Manchester Art School to study fashion design and management, afterwards going to work with Ib Jorgensen in Dublin. He was twenty-eight before he set up his own business, because time spent studying pattern-cutting in Belfast, a spell freelancing for English clothing companies and more study at St Martin's College in London all intervened. But eventually he could procrastinate no longer and settled in Dublin, where the quality of his work was immediately recognised. "When I started in 1978," he explains, "where I saw an opportunity was that up till then most ready-to-wear producers were more manufacturers turning out a suit, trousers and a skirt and they were all working from the same block. There was this incredible similarity between all of their work. So I felt there was an opportunity to start a ready-to-wear business for somebody whose background was in design, so that you'd be a designer-manufacturer as opposed to just a manufacturer."

At the start of his solo career, it appeared he could make no mistakes. Having begun the business in one room cutting his own patterns and with a single machinist, by 1980 he had annual sales in the region of £150,000 and climbing by 40 per cent each year. He was exporting to other European countries and had been given orders by a number of New York department stores including Macy's, Bloomingdale's and Barney's. In the *Irish Press*, Carolyn Donnelly in 1981 suggested his work possessed "a timeless quality that appeals to American women. And with the current trend towards simple stylish clothes (epitomised by designers like Calvin Klein and Perry Ellis) sweeping the States, everything seems to be in Michael's favour." A year later, in the *Cork Examiner*, the

ABOVE Coats are the garments for which Michael Mortell has been best known since the onset of his career. This example, in black nylon, dates from around 1984 when the designer was at the very height of his fame in Ireland and had opened shops in both Dublin and Brussels.

LEFT One of photographer Mike Bunn's most celebrated pictures for Michael Mortell, this dates from 1987 and shows both parties at their most effective. Mortell's black-based clothing acts as an inspiration for a shot in which the model's appearance looks both contemporary and yet reminiscent of an earlier era.

Dating from the mid-1980s, this outfit shows Michael Mortell's increasing interest in a more complex silhouette than he had produced before. Notice how the jacket and matching waistcoat have asymmetrical fastenings, in line with a universal response to the new school of Japanese fashion design then coming to prominence.

designer was estimating the retail value of his exports to the United States to be in the region of $200,000.

Michael Mortell's greatest gift lay in his ability to produce contemporary but commercial clothing with exceptionally good tailoring. From the start, his coats have been the most critically admired part of his collections. In the early seasons, for example, he produced enormously popular shower-proof quilted jackets trimmed in leather. Later, he offered leather-trimmed trench coats which became best-sellers and long tweed coats using fabric from McNutt's and Connemara Tweeds. These were sold in the Mirror, Mirror chain, the owner of which, Muriel Kerr, was among the very first retailers to recognise Michael Mortell's talents. But even while he used local fabrics, reflecting the changes Ireland's fashion industry had been forced to make during the 1970s, his finished clothes were never identifiably Irish in character. "When I design," he told the *Cork Examiner* in November 1981, "I try to create an international look…Anyway, I don't think such a thing as an 'Irish' design exists. I have used leather and tweed trimmings on my coats and if people like the tweed, then that's a plus for Ireland but it's not the critical factor."

By this time, he had won the Late, Late Designer of the Year for the first time along with a host of other accolades. A year later, his clothing was being stocked in Harrods in London and he had opened his own outlet in Brussels; this was followed in September 1984 by a Michael Mortell shop in Dublin. A profile in the *Sunday Independent* by Anne Harris earlier that year described the designer as "showing the craft of a master. His trenchcoats are now classics, a part of the vocabulary of fashion." But the same writer noticed a change in the character of the clothes being produced; instead of strongly-tailored garments, Michael Mortell's designs were being heavily influenced by the Japanese school then starting to make its presence felt in Europe. His work became softer and less highly structured; there was more emphasis on layering and contrast between surface textures. By September 1985, the *Irish Times* could report that his latest collection "was a complete break from the kind of thing Mortell has perfected over the years. For a start it was colourful; for another, there were extraordinary new fabrics; and most surprising of all, there was no tweed."

Today he reflects, "I did have a problem in the eighties because

I had too many heroes. One season I'd do an ode to Renaissance Italy using big brocade fabrics and shiny satin which was very beautiful. The next season I might have jumped onto the Japanese peasant look with crinkled fabric, completely unstructured baggy trousers and asymmetric fronts. And then after that I was probably doing my puritan Shaker look in black and white. I think I was giving the buyers a hard time because the great success of designers is an evolution of their own individual style. In fashion, one should be slightly tunnel vision in one's taste to be a great designer."

Michael Mortell seems never to have relished the demands of producing a twice-yearly collection. In 1984, he told the *Irish Times* that designing was something he found very demanding because "I hate the treadmill, having to stay awake visually, working without any room for mistakes". In the late 1980s, tiring of being a retailer, he closed his shops in Dublin and Brussels and began to specialise in coats. "One day in 1990," he now remembers, "I was sitting in my workroom wondering what would I do next season. I noticed all the rails of garments going out were loaded with raincoats and I thought, Michael, there's something nudging your shoulder here and maybe you should concentrate on that. At the time, I felt very burnt-out personally and tired. I thought maybe if I gave myself a break for a few years without actually leaving the business and specialised in something I found easier to do, that I'd be better off. And when and if I felt like going back to fashion, I'd have the strength and the business to do it." Sadly, Michael Mortell has not yet chosen to go back to fashion, although he does run a very successful raincoat manufacturing company selling both in Ireland and overseas. Still, his talent is a loss Irish fashion can ill afford and it can only be hoped that one day he returns to a field in which he was once master.

John Rocha

What has endured from that period is his friendship with another designer, John Rocha. In Britain, where he won the Designer of the Year award in 1993, Rocha is certainly the best-known designer based in Ireland. Yet curiously, he was neither born in the country nor is his parentage Irish. His mother is Chinese, his father

Portuguese and he grew up in Hong Kong. His arrival in Ireland was due to a chance meeting with a young Irish designer Eily Doolin (later his first wife) when they were both studying fashion at Croydon College of Art in England. "I used to come to Ireland during the summer holidays," he now recalls. "In fact, I started my fashion career by selling second-hand clothes in the Dandelion Market in Dublin." After graduation, the couple moved in 1978 to Kilkenny where, initially based in a garage, they produced complementary lines, his being mainly daywear, hers evening and wedding dresses. These began to be stocked by both Irish and British retailers and, following a move to Dublin, he soon had an annual turnover in the region of £500,000. In 1983 the Rocha/Doolin marriage ended and so, for a very brief time, did his business.

By March 1984, however, he was back with a new partner and muse, Odette Gleeson - whom he subsequently married - and a

"Over twenty years, I hope my work has improved from season to season," says John Rocha, "but I think the foundation has stayed very much the same...It's doing what will look well on the person." This 1986 collection would still look well today, with only the shoulder line betraying the date.

new label called Chinatown with its own outlet in Dublin's Powerscourt Townhouse Centre. From the start, Chinatown clothes were definitely not Irish in look; an *Irish Times* review of that first collection remarks of the trousers on sale, "they don't fit and were never supposed to". "Flamboyant, exciting, extreme and aggressively young," the notice continued, "it's also strongly oriental in flavour." That orientalism reflected the era's enthusiasm for clothes which were large, loose, layered and deconstructed. At the same time, if he has not shown much interest in the country's tradition of neat tailoring, awareness of a fabric's tactile possibilities and an enthusiasm for surface

Sybil Connolly was an unashamed romantic and yet there was great simplicity about her methods. Here is one of her timeless (and therefore impossible to date precisely) skirts and blouses, in the designer's signature pleated linen. Aside from a bow tied around the waist nothing else is used, and nothing else needed. (chapter two)

BELOW One of Irene Gilbert's most loyal clients was Anne, Countess of Rosse, who kept most of the clothes she had made for her. This scarlet taffeta ballgown dating from the early 1950s carries echoes of women's evening dress from a century earlier.

BOTTOM This cocktail ensemble in purple was designed for the Countess of Rosse in the early 1960s and is now preserved in the family home of Birr Castle, Co Offaly. Before her death in 1992, she carefully catalogued her collection, pinning personal reminiscences onto many garments. (chapter two)

Grace O'Shaughnessy, a popular model from the 1960s, here wears one of Neilli Mulcahy's most striking designs. The traditional dresser serves as a perfect backdrop for the high-necked orange tweed coat with its bands of double-welted stitching at the waist. (chapter three)

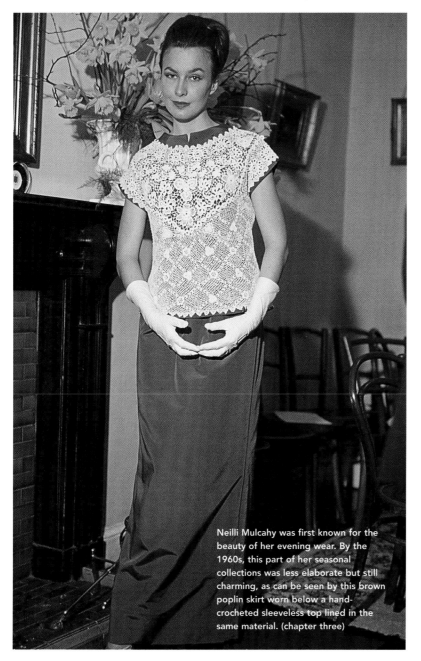

Neilli Mulcahy was first known for the beauty of her evening wear. By the 1960s, this part of her seasonal collections was less elaborate but still charming, as can be seen by this brown poplin skirt worn below a hand-crocheted sleeveless top lined in the same material. (chapter three)

RIGHT Mary O'Donnell says her clothes date so little that she risks putting herself out of business. This evening skirt and crochet top could still be worn today, almost thirty years after they were first made. Their beauty and simplicity testify to her training with the great American couturier Mainbocher. (chapter three)

TOP RIGHT Flowers are a recurring motif in Mary O'Donnell's work, as seen here on a skirt and blouse from the late 1960s. The satin skirt is hand-embroidered with clusters of white daisies while the top, in hand-crochet, is designed to imitate the floral pattern. (chapter three)

TOP: Fabulously embroidered item
such as this jacket were one of the
hallmarks of Ib Jorgensen's work
many years. By the time he open
studio at 24 Fitzwilliam Square in
late 1960s, he employed some 45
members of staff and was dressin
most of the wealthiest women in
Ireland. (chapter four)

ABOVE: Culottes were much in v
in the late 1970s and early 1980s
they were included in a wool win
pane check suit dating from autu
1981, designed by Ib Jorgensen.
love of detail may be seen in the
down the front of the jacket.
(chapter four)

MAIN: Many of Ib Jorgensen's m
spectacular examples of evening
incorporated designs by his wife
Patricia, as in this worsted wool c
cut on kimono lines and carrying
large applique of irises in pure si
from autumn 1975.
(chapter four)

ABOVE Sharon Bacon, Richard Lewis's favourite model, is here seen wearing one of his designs from 1979. Although the top uses his popular matt jersey, it is cut in a more dramatic and angular form than customary. (chapter four)

TOP Drama is achieved by a variety of means in this Richard Lewis two-piece dating from 1985. The rich colour helps, as does the contrast between the velvet of the skirt and the jacket's silk satin, but there is also the difference between the simple line of the lower piece and the gathered peplum above. (chapter four)

LEFT Rich colour, simple shapes and supple fabrics are the three elements which go into making Richard Lewis's clothes so distinctively his own. "Richard is a dressmaker in the very real sense of the word," fashion journalist Ruth Kelly once wrote. "He makes the most beautiful and flattering dresses." (chapter four)

The cardigan seems incapable of being given a new twist, but here, in the Rochas spring/summer 1993 collection, Peter O'Brien has simply reversed (and lengthened) the garment so that it now buttons at the back, allowing more flesh to be exposed. (chapter five)

TOP LEFT Peter O'Brien's evening wear often harks back to the 1930s and even earlier. This particular outfit from his Rochas autumn/winter 1994 range might almost be Edwardian in its lines and extravagant use of contrasting patterns; only the bare midriff confirms that it belongs to a much more recent era. (chapter five)

LEFT Anyone believing there is no life left in the Aran knit need only see this rhinestone-studded evening dress to realise how wrong they are. Designed by Peter O'Brien for the Rochas autumn/winter 1993 collection, the dress is now in the Ulster Museum in Belfast. (chapter five)

BOTTOM LEFT "Everyone says my colours are very Irish," observes Peter O'Brien, but sometimes his choice of fabrics can reveal his origins as well. Here from his autumn/winter 1995 collection for Rochas, for example, is a herringbone tweed jacket (and matching hat) worn over a crochet blouse. The former is given a touch of luxury by the embroidery above its left pocket. (chapter five)

Irish designer Jacqueline Quinn, based in New York working for an American clothing company, produced a collection under her own name in 1999. Its inspiration was the 1950s but, as this outfit shows, the designer wanted to update styles from that period rather than just plagiarise them. The funnel-necked sweater is embroidered with clusters of bugle beads to give it additional surface interest. (chapter five)

BOTTOM LEFT One of Lorcan Mullany's best-known customers was the late Diana, Princess of Wales. Here she is seen wearing a short cocktail dress, its black lace bodice embroidered with sequins beneath a white satin off-the-shoulder collar trimmed at the front with a black bow. (chapter five)

BOTTOM RIGHT "I like glamorous clothes," Lorcan Mullany explains. "I like them to be sexy but not overtly so. I like them to be refined. I suppose they're for women with a fairly big social life." This square-necked evening dress from the designer's winter 1998 collection certainly conforms to this description. (chapter five)

MAIN PICTURE "I always wanted to be a designer ever since I can remember and I always designed," comments Lorcan Mullany. But he can also produce high-quality drawings of the work he intends to make. This example is for the silver-grey evening dress seen in the photograph beside it. (chapter five)

Paul Costelloe is often described as Ireland's answer to Ralph Lauren and this very understated striped sweater and skirt do suggest a similarity. There is never anything fussy about Costelloe's work, and this explains his appeal to women who can bring their own personality to his clothes. (chapter six)

TOP LEFT "I wanted to bring the American philosophy of casual rather than rigid tailoring to the industry," is how Paul Costelloe describes his reason for setting up business in 1979. Twenty years later, as this soft-shouldered jacket and dress from the designer's autumn/winter 1999 collection make clear, he has remained true to his original ideas. (chapter six)

LEFT Paul Costelloe has said that with age the clothes he designs have become steadily less structured and more casual in character. That is certainly the case with this outfit from his menswear collection for spring/summer 1998 in which a trans-Atlantic spirit of relaxed ease is pre-eminent. (chapter six)

During the 1990s, Quin & Donnelly produced their collections to be sold in Ireland's A Wear chain, which explains why their designs have continued to be so reasonably priced. These velvet trousers and print top from the duo's autumn/winter 1999 collection, for example, were priced at £100 each. (chapter seven)

TOP LEFT In the mid-1980s, Quin & Donnelly began to reflect the Japanese interest in unstructured clothing. Because of its loose weave and softness, linen is particularly useful for such work, as can be seen in this pinafore dress and double-breasted jacket. (chapter seven)

Michael Mortell first came to public attention for the outstanding quality of his coats. This example from 1985 is typical of his designs from the period, in particular in its use of leather for the collar, echoed here by the matching trousers. (chapter seven)

LEFT Alison Doody, now better known as an actress, was a very young model in 1985 when she was photographed wearing this Michael Mortell sweater from the designer's autumn/winter collection. (chapter seven)

Louise Kennedy has always appreciated the customer's changing needs. While many women still want suiting with a well-defined silhouette, of late a demand for softer lines has begun to emerge and the designer has been happy to answer it, as shown by this piece from her spring/summer 1999 collection. (chapter seven)

TOP Impeccably tailored suiting has always been the cornerstone of a Louise Kennedy collection. This particular example comes from autumn/winter 1986; she had only been in business for a few seasons, but already it was clear she could produce clothes which have a strong personal signature but are not too radical in character. (chapter seven)

ABOVE "I design for women who want a streamlined look, rather than a definite fashion statement," Louise Kennedy said in 1998. This suit from her autumn/winter collection of 1997 confirms that statement, but the streamlined jacket and skirt possess drama thanks to their brilliant red colour. (chapter seven)

LEFT From Louise Kennedy's spring/summer 1992 collection, these simple pieces show the designer's preference for the colour blue and her awareness that understated clothes can be given additional authority through dramatic accessories. Model Cathy Lawson wears one of Kennedy's large, hand-painted shawls. (chapter seven)

ABOVE While she initially tended to concentrate on daywear, more recently Louise Kennedy has begun to create beautiful evening clothes. As this dress from her autumn/winter range shows, the designer's sense of authoritative understatement still prevails even if the purpose of the garment has changed. (chapter seven)

LEFT Bright colour is used unabashedly by John Rocha here for his autumn/winter 1996 menswear collection. If the colours and textures are unusual, the shapes are not and here lies the secret of the designer's success; he understands that the customer can only accept a certain degree of radicalism at any one time. (chapter seven)

ABOVE "It's very important for us to be proud of our traditions,"says John Rocha, "but also to bring them forward in a modern form." He does just that with a ribbed cardigan from his menswear collection for autumn/winter 1995; its colour and texture are reminiscent of the country's popular tweed jackets, but its form is contemporary especially when, as here, it is worn with a T-shirt. (chapter seven)

RIGHT When John Rocha first moved to Ireland in 1978, he specialised in knitwear, and that form has always retained a strong presence in his collections. Here model Naomi Campbell wears a white cotton cobweb-knit cardigan coat from his spring/summer 1994 range. (chapter seven.

ABOVE LEFT Asian designers such as John Rocha not only brought a new aesthetic to European fashion from the 1970s onwards, they also made black the most stylish of all colours. Here, from Rocha's spring/summer 1995 collection, is a dress in layered georgette that displays the merits of black to best advantage. (chapter seven)

ABOVE RIGHT A concern for surface decoration has always been important among Irish designers, even for those like John Rocha who did not grow up in the country. This devoré dress from his spring/summer 1997 collection demonstrates his continued pursuit of new means to give even the simplest of items additional visual interest. (chapter seven)

ABOVE Established in 1936, the Dublin shop Cleo enjoys an international reputation for the quality of its Aran sweaters, most hand-knitted to patterns which date back more than half a century. When Cleo first opened, such pieces sold for just a few pounds, but their price is now somewhat higher. (chapter eight)

RIGHT Cleo could be considered a bastion of traditional Irish style. Photographed outside the roofless ruin of Powerscourt House in County Wicklow, the foreground model is wearing a Munster cloak over a red Connemara skirt and white cotton blouse; the man behind wears an opera cape. (chapter eight)

LEFT Although she may no longer focus on knitwear, Pat Crowley still likes to use traditional Irish fabrics, as may be seen in this light tweed suit and matching cape. Clothes of this calibre sold as well to her American as to her Irish clients. (chapter eight)

ABOVE Many of Pat Crowley's most loyal customers have busy social lives, and she offered them lots of items such as this cocktail dress dating from 1985. The dropped waist and the net top covering the arms and swathing the neck in ruffles all indicate that the dress would particularly suit an older woman. (chapter eight)

RIGHT From her start on a domestic sewing machine in her home, Lynn Elliott has grown to enjoy considerable success in Ireland, Britain and elsewhere. From her autumn/winter 1999 collection for Lyn-Mar comes this long grey knit coat worn over a metallic chiffon pinafore dress with felt sweater and felt underskirt. (chapter eight)

LEFT One of Lainey Keogh's great skills lies in her ability to mix different textures with unexpected success. Here, for example, from her autumn/winter 1998 collection, she combines ribbed chenille and fur in the jacket which is then worn over a cobweb knit dress. (chapter eight)

FAR LEFT "Knitwear is a rather unlikely field for innovation, one might think," observes American Vogue's Hamish Bowles, "but Lainey is there to prove us wrong." One innovation for which this designer can claim credit is bringing a sense of sexiness to knits, as seen in this remarkably complex and simultaneously simple dress from her spring/summer 1998 collection. (chapter eight)

BELOW LEFT In February 1999, Lainey Keogh took over the main hall of London's Natural History Museum to stage her biggest and most critically acclaimed show to date. She waited many years, serving what she describes as her "apprenticeship", before choosing to stage shows but the response from retailers and customers around the world proves she was wise to wait. (chapter eight)

This brilliant red mohair cardigan helped to make Lainey Keogh a Late, Late Fashion Award winner in 1985, but bears little resemblance to the work she has since produced. Her early designs tended to be both very loose-fitting and have a lot of raised surface decoration, but little of the inherent sensuality she has subsequently brought to her work. (chapter eight)

RIGHT Commercial success has given Daryl Kerrigan many advantages; she no longer has to run up her clothes on a sewing machine at the back of her shop. She can use better fabrics and more sophisticated techniques, as here in a cap-sleeved shirt from her spring/summer 2000 collection. Some things remain consistent, however, such as the designer's devotion to hipster pants. (chapter nine)

BOTTOM RIGHT Daryl Kerrigan's hipster pants (seen here in a cropped version for spring 1999) first made her name in the United States. However the popularity of this design meant, as she admits, "our cut and pattern have been taken by other people; that's how fashion works and there's nothing you can do about it." (chapter nine)

BOTTOM LEFT The inherent conservatism of most American fashion houses undoubtedly helped Dubliner Daryl Kerrigan when she first launched a label under her own name in 1992. Five years later, when these clothes made their debut, she was awarded the Perry Ellis Award for Young Designer of the Year by the Council of Fashion Designers in America. (chapter nine)

OPPOSITE "His hats are all about incredible precision of construction and a really dramatic sense of craftmanship," says American Vogue's Hamish Bowles of Philip Treacy, adding "He's really a designer who pushes fashion forward even though he's not producing clothing." (chapter nine)

LEFT Paula Reed, from Northern Ireland, argues that Philip Treacy "has a very lyrical, romantic sense of shape and colour and style. That lyricism and romance absolutely come from his Irish background." Both qualities are clearly evident in this hat from the designer's 1998 collection. (chapter nine)

TOP LEFT Among the models participating in Philip Treacy's show in February 1999 was American singer/actress Grace Jones, seen here wearing one of the milliner's smaller, but no less dramatic than usual, hats from his millennial collection. (chapter nine)

TOP RUGHT Philip Treacy is as much an engineer as a designer since he must resolve extremely complex technical difficulties. A hat such as that shown here (from his collection for 1999) needs to be constructed from materials light enough not to cause the wearer discomfort and yet strong enough to survive repeated use. (chapter nine)

BELOW Less than half a century ago, Irish fashion was primarily practised by couturiers based in Dublin, even if they had an international clientele. Now only a handful of such designers continue in business, the youngest of them being Jen Kelly, from whose 1999 collection come this ice blue double crepe silk dress and printed silk coat. (chapter ten)

BELOW LEFT Couture tends to find its clientele today among women who are looking for clothes suiting some special occasion; therefore, daywear features less strongly. Couturiers such as Jen Kelly find the greatest demand is for items such as this scarlet bias-cut evening dress in silk crepe. (chapter ten).

ABOVE RIGHT As a child growing up on a farm in Co Tyrone, Sharon Wauchob says, "I was aware that a lot of the clothes I saw seemed to me to be getting it wrong and I kept hooking things up the side and playing with clothes." That interest in playing with the possibilities clothes offer (and hooking them up the side) remains with her, as this photograph makes clear. (chapter nine)

ABOVE LEFT Reluctant as she is to follow the now-stale format of the fashion show, Sharon Wauchob sticks with tradition because, she says, "my clothes work best when they're on women; there's a feeling of reality and movement. The show gives an understanding of my clothes." (chapter nine)

"Obviously, compared to women's clothes, menswear doesn't change rapidly from season to season," says Cuan Hanly. "Instead, there tends to be more innovation in the fabric that's used and the finish on it. So with my collections, I'm trying to keep them classic but contemporary and moving forward." (chapter ten)

Ireland's new generation of confident young professional women loves Marc O'Neill's clothes and this dress shows why. In black lace over a red base, it is simple, stylish and versatile enough to suit a wide range of occasions. (chapter ten)

OVERLEAF Although his greatest strength lies in immaculate tailoring, there is also a streak of romanticism running through Marc O'Neill's character which occasionally finds an outlet in his work, as here in a long-sleeved sheer top and corset-fronted A-line skirt. (chapter ten)

Simple shapes in luxurious fibres are the essence of Lucy Downes's range of knitwear; for her debut collection, she used cashmere, in a variety of colours ranging from the sober to the vibrant. (chapter ten)

embellishment – two qualities consistently identified by observers as typical of Irish fashion – have been much in evidence in John Rocha's work for the past twenty years.

A profile of the designer in the *Sunday Press* in February 1990 noted that his spring/summer collection would be using more than 35,000 metres of Irish linen, and he has constantly used tweed in his lines for both men and women. Moreover, the inherent character of his work is Irish, as American *Vogue's* Hamish Bowles notes when he says, "although John wasn't born in Ireland, I think he's certainly absorbed the influence and history of Irish dress into what he does. He's used fabrics and the country's rather romantic sensibility but overlaid that with something eastern and Zen-like. His starting point might have been with the Japanese like Yohji Yamamoto and Rei Kawakubo of Commes Garcons with their iconoclastic approach to design and turning clothing inside out but he has layered it into something more artsy and poetical. The structure has its roots in the east but the fabrics and application are very much Irish."

John Rocha has frequently used Celtic motifs on his garments, either embroidered or hand-painted onto the surface, and he even gives Irish names to collections; that for autumn/winter 1993, for example, was called Dochas (meaning hope). "It's very important for us to be proud of our traditions," he says, "but also to bring them forward in a modern form. So what I do when I look at something old and wonderful is to give it a twist to make it slightly different. Over the years, I've done this in hand-painting, in embellishment, in beading. Every season, something I've seen through the years is subconsciously coming back." From his earliest days with Chinatown, the designer's very individual alliance of eastern and western clothing cultures has stayed largely unaltered. As Hamish Bowles remarks, "John has remained true to himself; he has gone with a certain lyrical deconstructed craft approach and has honed that over the seasons. He's an evolutionary rather than a revolutionary designer." John Rocha would agree with this summation, saying "Over twenty years, I hope my work has improved from season to season but I think the foundations have stayed very much the same."

What changed on a number of occasions were the designer's own circumstances. Despite critical success, the economic

When John Rocha joined forces with the A Wear chain in the late 1980s, he had to produce work which was capable of mass-production but still contained clear evidence of the designer's distinctive style – no easy task. Here, in 1991, he succeeds completely in this objective, thanks to the elaborate ruching on the front of the jacket and the generous folds of its hood.

problems continuing to dog Irish fashion meant that in January 1988 John Rocha had to close his manufacturing business, owing more than £300,000; it is a measure of his personal popularity that one creditor at the time described him as "very honourable". After this second setback, he appeared to lose heart and left Ireland to work in Milan, but within six months he was producing a range under the Chinatown label for the A Wear chain and eventually returned to live and work in Dublin. Thereafter, his ascent has been steady; by the time he won the British Designer of the Year award in October 1993, he was selling the Chinatown label not just to Irish consumers but to twenty-one other countries as well with annual exports worth in the region of £2 million.

Even when he parted company from A Wear a year after his win in London, thanks to backing from his wife's brothers he continued to expand. Many of Ireland's best-known performers are both friends and admirers of his work, which has been modelled in the past by Bob Geldof and Sinead O'Connor. He designs twice-yearly collections for men and women, shown in Paris and London respectively, as well as a more casual line, John Rocha Jeans, for both sexes. He has had his own shop in central London but is stocked by department stores and shops throughout Britain. Extremely popular, John Rocha is liked for the warmth of his character as well as the quality of his designs. In May 1997, he moved into the field of home furnishings, producing a range of tableware for Waterford Crystal which proved to be phenomenally successful; in its first year, sales were twice what had been predicted. Since then, he has been responsible for designing the interior decoration of Dublin's Morrison Hotel, opened in July 1999.

John Rocha may have experienced difficulties during the 1980s when he was finding his feet, but since then he has learnt to concentrate on designing and leave the rest of the business to others. "Fashion is like a four-legged table," he said in 1996. "You need a good designer, a very good business manager, a good manufacturer and a very good distributor. Without all the legs, the table collapses." Collapse now seems less likely; John Rocha's annual turnover in 1999 was in the region of £5 million, with exports accounting for 80 per cent of his business. Britain is his biggest market outside Ireland. He demonstrates that a fashion designer can be based in Dublin and still enjoy an international career.

LEFT **It is easy to imagine that because John Rocha is a successful designer, he does not need to understand the requirements of the average customer. Yet in every collection there is a selection of items, such as this suit dating from 1991, which are simple, practical and easy to mix with other pieces.**

Louise Kennedy

Another designer whose career also began in the 1980s, who lives in Dublin but enjoys a healthy export business, is Louise Kennedy. She differs from Rocha, however, in that her clothes have little of the overt Irish sensibility seen in his work. Two other features distinguish her from other designers in Ireland: in an industry where successful women were once a commonplace, she is now something of a rarity, and she is also much more articulate than many of her peers. Born in 1960, Louise Kennedy comes from a retail background in Thurles, County Tipperary where her mother owned a drapery shop. Following the latter's death in 1984, she returned home from Dublin where she had studied fashion at the Grafton Academy of Dress Design. While running the family business, she continued to produce her own work, selling it to a number of outlets in the capital. It seemed possible that she might remain in Thurles but eventually the shop there was sold, not without a wrench since it had been in her maternal family for a century.

Louise Kennedy returned to Dublin, where she has been based ever since. Looking back to the early days, she credits her mother with her first interest in design, saying of her, "she had a great feeling for fabrics, always looked elegant and had a meticulous eye for detail". This could just as easily be a description of Louise Kennedy herself particularly since, from the beginning, her clothes were noted for their impeccable finish. An early review from November 1986 in the *Irish Times* observed that she wore her own designs "with head-turning effect" – she has always been her own best model - and summarised the clothes as "restrained and carefully tailored".

Restraint and tailoring of the highest quality have traditionally been the hallmarks of Louise Kennedy's work. She may be considered to have inherited the mantle of those designers in Ireland during the 1970s and earlier who had first begun to produce smart suiting for professional women; as the latter's numbers have steadily climbed during the 1990s, so too has her market. "I design for women who want a streamlined look, rather than a definite fashion statement," she remarked in 1998, her clientele being "women who have a great sense of knowing what

LEFT When John Rocha showed his clothes during London Fashion Week in the mid-1980s, this menswear collection was among the earliest pieces to catch overseas buyers' eyes. The shapes and proportions are no longer fashionable, but the fabrics – especially the use of rich Irish tweed seen in the jacket – have remained a constant presence in the designer's work.

suits them and don't need labels to boost their confidence." For much of the last decade, the Irish woman who best defined that sense of self-awareness and confidence was the country's president, Mary Robinson, who had been dressed by Louise Kennedy for her inauguration in December 1990 and thereafter regularly bought clothes from the designer. So too has her successor, Mary McAleese, as well as such well-known figures as Cherie Blair, wife of the British Prime Minister, former American ambassador to Ireland Jean Kennedy Smith and a large number of actresses and singers.

"Louise Kennedy's very successful because her product is very good," says Andrew Tucker. "What she has done is design relaxed, elegant career wear for working women which is now her hallmark; it's the office suit executed in beautiful fabrics and with supreme quality. The way she designs is all about little elements that bring a garment to life. That has nothing to do with her being Irish – she's a good designer and that's all there is to it." Louise Kennedy customers can be confident that they will be acquiring comfortable, well-produced clothes which avoid the extremes of fashion. As the *Sunday Tribune's* Deirdre McQuillan wrote in February 1995, "These are quiet, refined clothes that don't need to shout their qualities. Like the designer herself." While the work is usually very tailored, Louise Kennedy tends to avoid the impression of excessive masculinity by adding such elements as a hand-painted scarf or a devoré shawl. All these features were evident in the staff uniforms she designed for Aer Lingus in 1997.

In the late 1990s her collections began to become notably softer and more youthful in character as she made shoulderlines less defined and the entire silhouette of her suiting and coats much gentler in outline. The fabrics she has always preferred to use assist in this process; Louise Kennedy has been a keen fan of fluid Italian weaves such as those used by Giorgio Armani. These light, luxurious materials work well with other elements in her range such as fine-weight shearling jackets and coats and cashmere knits; for spring/summer she has regularly included linen pieces. Like Armani also, her evening wear is inclined to combine simple shapes with elaborate beading; the drama is achieved by the surface pattern rather than by the garment's cut. Her colour palette also grew more delicate towards the end of the 1990s; while she has almost never worked with prints, her choice of colouring initially tended to be rather dark. More recently, she has opted instead for pale, honey shades and pastels.

This impression of subdued luxury is evident also in the decoration of the Merrion Square house which became Louise Kennedy's headquarters in October 1998, just as it had been designer Raymond Kenna's over forty years earlier. Here she opened a retail outlet carrying not only her full range of goods but complementary items such as hats by Philip Treacy and bags by Lulu Guinness. In what has been described as Ireland's "smallest and smartest department shore", the retailing experience of her youth has stood her in good stead. And, like Paul Costelloe and John Rocha, she has expanded her interests to include homeware, beginning with a range of glasses, vases and candlesticks for Tipperary Crystal. Like her clothing, these items have an elegant fluidity and manage to be both attractive and functional. In many respects, Louise Kennedy is an atypical Irish designer. Although items such as her hand-painted scarves and linen dresses woven with a floral pattern indicate an interest in surface texture, she is as much Italian as Irish in her inspiration and sensibility. Unusual as this cosmopolitan flavour in an Irish designer's work might have appeared during earlier decades, it was increasingly to become the norm as the century drew to a close.

knitwear: 1950–99

By in its very nature, fashion is incapable of ever staying still. Because the industry has to be simultaneously creative and commercial, it must always produce fresh ideas for the consumer. Otherwise sales are liable to fall and the designer's business collapse. And yet, in contradiction to this customary pattern, one area of Irish fashion has shown itself to be both resistant to change and highly successful in the market. That area is knitwear in which, for much of the 20th century, tradition rather than innovation has been much prized.

"Knitwear's an interesting phenomenon," agrees Elizabeth McCrum. For her, among the form's most arresting characteristics is the fact that anyone in possession of a ball of wool and two needles can take up knitting. However, "You can also take advantage of the most advanced technology. The strength of Irish knitwear, I think, is that Irish designers have used both elements. There's still a very strong hand-crafted quality in the work of many of them, but high technology is also producing the economic qualities of knitwear which have made it such a vital force in Irish fashion abroad." There can be no doubt that knitwear includes many of the elements which commentators, Irish and non-Irish alike, have suggested are most representative of the country's fashion. As Elizabeth McCrum points out, it possesses a strong hand-crafted quality and in addition, tends to depend on surface texture and the play of colour and pattern for its interest. All these are features which, while not exclusive to knitwear in Ireland, certainly appear particularly well developed here.

There are additional reasons why knitting should have found such an enthusiastic welcome in Ireland. An obvious one is practical; the country has always produced wool and so the native population tended to make knitted goods. "It's very much part of our history," says Irish fashion writer and author of *The Aran Sweater*, Deirdre McQuillan. "We've been knitting since the 17th century, although mostly socks it has to be said." She also comments on the social nature of knitting, as an activity that can be done by groups of women together, and points out that during the 1940s and 1950s the Irish Countrywomen's Association held knitting competitions around the country "which encouraged knitwear design and fostered an interest in the whole form".

The interest was often greater overseas than at home. Irish

knitwear has always played an important part in clothing exports. Coras Tráchtála from the beginning was keen to sell the country's sweaters overseas and as early as 1952, some £25,000 worth of Irish knitwear was being exported. Since then, the market abroad has steadily grown, although like most other sectors it did experience something of a setback during the difficult years of the 1970s. The 1990s were a particularly good decade for this area of Irish clothing exports. In 1991, the total value of Irish knitwear sold overseas stood at £35 million; by 1998 that figure had more than doubled to £73.4 million. Enterprise Ireland's Regional Director in Europe, Jim Maguire, confirms, "Knitwear is a key export product and in fact it's practically synonymous with Ireland. A lot of Europeans think the sheep is the Irish national animal. Of course, it's a certain kind of knitwear that's successful; it's heavy, primarily for outdoors and made in wool."

Aran sweaters

One particular form of knitwear has come to be seen as intrinsically Irish: the Aran sweater. While this may appear to have an ancient pedigree, in fact, like Irish Coffee, the Aran is a twentieth-century invention fortunate enough to acquire instant antiquity. Taking their name from the group of remote islands off the Galway coast, the precise origins of these sweaters are unclear; certainly, at the end of the 19th century the Aran islanders – while possessors of a distinctive style of dress - were not wearing knitted garments with intricate and elaborate stitching patterns. It is interesting to note, for example, that Robert Flaherty's 1934 film, "Man of Aran", depicting daily life on the island of Inishmore, does not feature a single Aran sweater. Even by that period, however, the sweater had begun to evolve and was starting to take the form in which it is now known worldwide. It took only a few decades after 1900 for this process to be completed.

This cotton knit by Tarlach de Blacam's Inis Meain shows that the Aran sweater need not be a fossilised item of clothing incapable of change. The complex arrangement of patterned stitches is of fundamental importance (Inis Meain has registered its own design) but just as important are shape and fibre, both of which are constantly subject to re-examination.

The most commonly accepted explanation for the origins of the Aran sweater are that it grew out of the knitting techniques shown to islanders by fishermen and their families from Scotland, Donegal and the Channel Islands; the presence of these seasonal visitors was encouraged by the Congested Districts Board, a government body set up in 1893 to reduce poverty in densely-populated areas of the country. But, as Deirdre McQuillan observes in her book on the subject, "The difference between Aran sweaters with their vertical panels of pattern and the many other fine examples of fishing ganseys from around England and Scotland of the time is the sheer exuberance of the Irish design. Like musical notation, once the knitters knew the notes and chords, they could make their own arrangements, compose their own music." The patterns created by the islanders were often examples of imaginative virtuosity. "Always with Irish fashion, there's a love for the tactile, for the embellishment of simple shapes," observes Elizabeth McCrum. "What Aran sweaters could give to knitwear was just that – the encrustation of the diamond, the cabling, all the stitches were something very stimulating." Deirdre McQuillan believes the Aran sweater's enduring appeal "lies in its simplicity and the textural relief patterns; like brocade, there's a depth of texture in just one colour. Because it began as an item of daily workwear, the form is so simple but the interest comes from decoration and texture."

Regrettably, many Aran sweaters sold today show little of the exuberance which distinguished their predecessors; patterns have become stereotyped and drained of the energy with which they were first produced. "I think Ireland has failed to update its traditions in terms of fashion," former editor of *Vogue Hommes* Godfrey Deeny observes. "Irish knitwear has a big reputation, but it has suffered historically from a lack of really talented designers going into it. Few things irritate me more than going into boutiques like Ralph Lauren or Calvin Klein and seeing them make Irish-style sweaters in yarns that maybe aren't as good as we have in Ireland but cutting them better so that the garments are more flattering and correspond to what's in right now. Then I go back to Ireland and try on a sweater and it immediately creates a tyre around my middle because it's cut all wrong. It's as if designers at home haven't left their studio to see how sweaters are being made elsewhere." Alternatively, perhaps the problem is simply that Aran sweaters were never intended to be fashion garments and their potential as such has still not been seen in Ireland.

The first generation of Aran knitters, for example, knew nothing about standard sizing, which caused serious problems when initial attempts were made to develop an export market for the garment. From the mid-1930s onwards, Arans began to be produced for sale thanks to the work of a handful of people outside the islands. Among these were the lawyer and writer Padraig Ó Síocháin; Padraig Ó Máille who had a tailoring and dress-making shop in Galway; the founder of the Country Shop in Dublin, Dr Muriel Gahan; and another Dublin retailer, Catherine Ryan, who opened an outlet called Cleo in 1936. Her daughter, Kitty Joyce, who still runs the business today, remembers that Aran sweaters were first included among Cleo's stock during the Second World War when most items of clothing were rationed and sales depended on coupons; for some reason, the hand-knitted sweaters being produced by the islanders were not subject to such restrictions. They were sold for £2 or £3 each and would be advertised not in fashion publications but in magazines read by fishermen in Britain and Ireland. Although it has moved premises several times, Cleo continues to be known for the wide range of Aran sweaters it carries and sells in the region of 1,500 such garments annually. These are produced by a group of more than 100 knitters working in their own homes and often using designs dating back to the 1940s.

Running an international business on a small island off the west coast of Ireland demands that Inis Meain pays attention to customers' demands. One of these is an interest in lighter fibres, such as the linen mix used for this cardigan. The company has also begun to produce garments made from luxurious yarns such as silk, cashmere and baby alpaca.

When Pat Crowley started her own business in 1968, having worked with Irene Gilbert for eight years, she specialised in traditional Irish crafts such as knitwear and crochet, given a contemporary look. This evening dress from 1970 is typical of her early collections.

Inis Meain

At least ninety per cent of Cleo's Aran sweaters are sold to tourists visiting Ireland; "Indigenous craft tends to be more appreciated by outsiders," is Kitty Joyce's explanation for the want of interest among the domestic market for Aran hand-knits. The same thought also occurs to Tarlach de Blacam who, on the Aran island of Inismaan, has spent almost a quarter century reinterpreting the traditional sweater for a contemporary market. His business, Inis Meain Knitting Company Ltd, has always been export-driven and today sends almost ninety-five per cent of everything it produces overseas, with the United States and Japan being its two biggest markets. "I always felt when we were first starting from our remote location with such expenses and overheads that we'd have to aim at the top end of the market," he says. "I wasn't sure that Ireland then had the large affluent population which could afford such an expensive product. But that's now changed, there is a wealthy population here and we need to start looking harder at the domestic market."

The company was set up in 1976, he explains, "as part of a co-operative project and as part of the development on the island to provide services and employment." Having begun with six knitters working on old domestic machines in a shed, the company now has its own factory, employs some twenty people (approximately ten per cent of Inismaan's population) and uses state-of-the-art machinery programmed to work twenty hours a day creating luxurious knitwear. Inis Meain may once have offered Aran knits in heavy unbleached wool, but today those sweaters are more likely to come in blends of alpaca, silk and cashmere. Just as importantly, the company produces a new collection twice-yearly like any other international fashion house.

With an annual turnover of just over £1 million, Inis Meain manufactures in the region of 15,000 garments a year. Although much of what is produced by this island-based business may not appear to have a connection with the traditional Aran sweater, some pieces in each range still show their origins. "Right through our collections there are various hand-writings from traditional knitters' designs," Tarlach de Blacam explains, "but we've one specific combination that we thought was very beautiful and we've registered that in the United States. We aim to make that specifically ours and gain a certain amount of recognition for it. The name Aran is almost a generic thing; it's such a shame the islanders couldn't capitalise on it in the same way the French have done on the regions of their wines because I feel strongly that the Aran stitch and pattern which was devised by different knitters on the islands has been stereotyped and bastardised around the world." It could be argued that Inis Meain's sweaters are not pure Aran designs either; after all, they are usually made in yarns other than wool and, while finished by hand, are primarily produced by machines. However, "I don't really get hung up on the dichotomy between hand-knitted garments and those created by machinery," says Tarlach de Blacam. "The most important thing for us is quality and styling and after that, we'll use whatever tools are available to us."

Pat Crowley

Inis Meain shows that it is possible to devise a successful marriage between the traditional and the contemporary. In the late 1960s and early 1970s, a number of designers such as Clodagh had already attempted just such a union, with varying degrees of success. Another member of this group was the late Agnes Bernelle, then known as Agnes Leslie, who for a few seasons ran a small cottage industry from County Monaghan called Castle Shane. The style of her hand-knits, according to a review in the *Irish Times* in June 1970, "was certainly young and casual" featuring such pieces as mini skirts and heavily fringed ponchos. These were made up in heavy wool with relatively plain patterns but bold colours such as turquoise. While this particular business did not survive long, it indicates that designers were

BELOW In the early 1970s, trouser suits for women became fashionable and Pat Crowley produced her own highly successful interpretation with a knitted cardigan jacket and matching flared pants. Both pieces incorporate that fundamental of the Aran sweater, the cable stitch, but thanks to their youthful silhouette and rich colouring they look anything but staid.

BELOW LEFT By 1971 not everyone wanted to wear the mini length, especially if they were paying eighteen guineas for a garment which was described by one journalist as "the handknitting equivalent of haute couture". The dense knit of this Pat Crowley dress is relieved by a more open crochet weave for the sleeves and around the neckline, demanding greater skill on the part of the worker.

ABOVE **A strikingly good-looking woman with rich auburn hair, Pat Crowley has consistently looked well in her own clothes. From the mid-1970s onwards, she began to introduce other items besides knitwear, and specialised in immaculately-finished dresses and suits similar to the pieces in silk poplin she is seen wearing here.**

RIGHT **Originally from Italy, Michelina Stacpoole often seems to be inspired by France. That is certainly the case with this outfit from 1973, a year after she had set up business under her own name. The striped cardigan and matching sweater beneath look as fresh today as when they were first designed.**

trying to find a means of maintaining a traditional Irish craft while taking cognisance of changing taste.

In her efforts to combine the familiar with the new, Pat Crowley can be seen as typical of the new movement in Irish knitwear during this period. Having worked for Irene Gilbert, she set up her own business in 1968 and concentrated on producing knits. One of her outfits was shown in the October edition of *Harper's Bazaar* that year and demonstrated that she was happy to take advantage of her Irish credentials while still giving consumers something new; the ensemble consisted of a dark emerald green crochet-knit A-line dress over cuffed trousers and worn with a lighter green jacket. Earlier in June 1968, her first collection was described by Terry Keane in the *Irish Times* as being "brilliant in colour, simple in design and examples of Irish designing talent at its very best". While the items were relatively expensive for the time – eighteen guineas for a dress and thirty-five guineas for a coat – these prices were justified, according to Terry Keane, because the pieces were "the handknitting equivalent of haute couture". Pat Crowley's early work tended to use designs in her garments which, although seemingly contemporary and abstract, owed their origins to established Aran patterns and forms adapted from the Book of Kells. But she also liked to include the Greek key pattern knitted into pieces in a strong contrasting shade to the main colour. Her forms were deliberately not traditional – sleeveless waistcoat tops, maxi skirts and long cardigan coats.

In March 1969, the *New York Times* proclaimed that her work "combines the appeal of the cottage industry with a highly civilized sense of colour and style". She used only pure fibres and all her work was hand-made by a team of more than one hundred handknitters based around the country. "We have a certain number of knitters who work at home," she told *Women's Wear Daily* in October 1971. "It takes up to six months before a woman becomes sufficiently skilled in knitting to meet our standards…They knit for the creative satisfaction it gives them, and the feeling they are doing something that calls for pride in craftsmanship." In the early 1970s, it was still possible to find such women prepared to work for relatively small amounts of money; in the same feature, Pat Crowley remarked that the average weekly earnings for her knitters were £4 or £5. By 1970 she was already so successful, thanks to large orders from American department stores, that she was able to open her own premises in Dublin at 36 Molesworth Street. But as the cost of producing hand-knits rose and the demand for such clothing proportionately fell, she started to design collections in other fabrics and soon knitwear featured as only one element of each season's range. Pat Crowley retired in Spring 2000.

Michelina Stacpoole

The nature of her knits became far less overtly ethnic. The same is also true of another designer in this field who began her career around the same time as Pat Crowley. Of course, if Michelina Stacpoole's knits do not display a strong Irish character, this may be explained by her Italian origins. Born near Naples, she came to Ireland to learn English and stayed in the country after setting up a fashion company in 1968. Initially she worked with a partner, but ventured out on her own in 1972 and has remained working from Adare, County Limerick ever since. From the start, Michelina Stacpoole's knits, rather like the tailored suits of Peter Fitzsimons and Patrick Howard during the same period, intentionally reflected international rather than local trends. She always

liked to use pure wool yarns and her preference was for simple, streamlined shapes given interest by bold stripes or by surface variation in the knit through ribbing and herringbone stitching. A May 1979 feature on Michelina Stacpoole in the *Irish Times* remarked that "It is on the pattern and texture that the designer spends much of her time, though her feeling for colour takes some beating". In many ways her work is reminiscent of that created by French knitwear designer Sonia Rykiel, another woman who knows how to make an impact by the simplest means.

A small team of local women has been responsible for producing the designs and this means that output remains relatively small. "I do not have computers knitting my clothes," she announced firmly to the *Irish Times* in March 1987, because "that gives a dull look." More than a decade later, she explained to the same newspaper, "As you know, you have to be something of a technician but with my workers I sometimes don't even have to draw a sketch." Her clothing has never been subject to radical changes and many customers continue to wear the same Stacpoole items for many years. This can certainly hinder future sales and she has had problems in the past, having to face liquidation in January 1988, the same time as John Rocha's Chinatown also closed down. However, a loyal clientele both in Ireland and the United States has allowed her to continue in business and she may now be compared to Thomas Wolfangel, another non-Irish designer long resident in Ireland.

Lynn Elliott

In the 1970s, Michelina Stacpoole's approach to knitwear suggested that traditional Irish forms such as the Aran sweater were gradually losing their vitality and would soon stagnate as no more than a tourist item. While this is certainly true in certain sections of the market, the success of a company like Inis Meain proved that there was fresh life yet in the Aran, even if produced on machines rather than by individual knitters. What was even more surprising in the 1990s was the resurgence of the hand-knit in Ireland, thanks to a number of designers who managed to give the work a new twist. Lynn Elliott is typical of this group. A mother of three based in County Meath, she began her career in 1987 based in her own

Based in Adare, Co Limerick, it is inevitable that Michelina Stacpoole's business should show some acknowledgement of Ireland's knitwear tradition. While the simple scoop-neck top may be international in character, the skirt quite clearly pays homage to Irish crochet with its bands of open weave. Dating from 1976, the clothes are worn by a popular Irish model of the period, Jean O'Reilly.

home, producing chunky sweaters on a domestic knitting machine. Initially the pieces were made as a hobby but her business, called Lyn-Mar, grew rapidly so that by 1993 she was the recipient of the Late, Late Show's fashion award for knitwear and, four years later, was chosen as the same event's Designer of the Year.

Although she now features other fabrics, knitwear remains at the centre of each Lyn-Mar collection using luxurious yarns like mohair and silk in rich shades. Her work, particularly the evening and bridal wear incorporating gold and silver thread, is highly romantic in spirit and has the qualities of softness and surface embellishment which are so common among Irish designers.

Lainey Keogh

While Lynn Elliott has become well-known in her own country, the designer who has single-handedly given Irish knitwear an international profile – and shown that this area of fashion can reflect the past yet be completely contemporary – is Lainey Keogh. There can be no doubt she is one of the most original talents to have emerged in Ireland's fashion industry during the past half century. As Hamish Bowles observes, "Knitwear is a rather unlikely field for innovation, one might think, but Lainey is there to prove us wrong. She took a craft and pushed it forward. She also found this way of expressing her own maverick sensibility on the knitting loom and created something that's proved enduringly exciting. For me, she is a quintessentially Irish designer even though she has put her imprimatur on international fashion. The whole organic quality of her work, the colour palette, the sense of craft and the poeticism I find all very Irish."

Everything about Lainey Keogh's career in fashion is unexpected, not least its origins. One of ten children of a North Dublin market gardener, she studied microbiology at university and after graduation worked in a hospital laboratory. Her first commissioned sweater was a piece she made for a man with whom she was in love and although the romance did not last, the interest in knitwear proved more abiding. In 1984, Michael Mortell asked her to make some items for inclusion in his own collection and she chose to give up her job to design full-time, initially selling work through the Irish Design Centre. During this period, the sweaters she made tended

She began by working only in knitwear, but Lynn Elliott of Lyn-Mar has since diversified into a wider range of clothing. Her style remains intensely romantic, as seen in this heavily beaded evening dress from autumn/winter 1998. The feathers on its shoulder straps are echoed by those on the accompanying wrap.

to reflect the heritage of the Aran sweater and of Celtic Ireland, seen in her preference for heavy yarns and simple bold designs. The shapes were predominantly large and loose. What changed in the 1990s was both the form and the fibre as she moved into lighter weights and more figure-hugging designs. Instead of just offering sweaters, she started to include coats, dresses and a wide range of other pieces. While she gradually built up demand for her clothes at home and abroad, it was more than a decade after her design debut before Lainey Keogh chose to stage her own solo show at London Fashion Week. "You do your apprenticeship and learn your craft," she explained to the *Irish Times* in February 1998. "A lot of people can get into the show thing far too early. It's important to know yourself and what you do before you go out there."

In the immediate aftermath of the first London show in February 1997, Lainey Keogh's international reputation really began to soar. For many members of the audience, that event – at which actor John Hurt recited poetry and the soundtrack of U2's new album was played – was a revelation of knitwear's potential. Afterwards, the *Daily Telegraph* wrote that the designer had "produced a fantastical array of hand-knits, patterned in textures as thick as honeycombs and as light as a spider's web". "It was quirky and unique," remembers Hamish Bowles, "because she used it as a showcase for the experiments she'd been doing – using metal filaments, simulating organic textures and substances through knitwear. What's exciting about Lainey is that she's always pushing the boundaries on what's technically possible. She has been able to take knitwear into a new dimension by working with yarns technically as well as creatively." This marriage of technology and creativity is what set the designer apart and allowed her to make a highly individual contribution to fashion.

In the second half of the 1990s, Lainey Keogh began to co-operate with Italian manufacturers – who she once described as being "like alchemists because they can create something from nothing" – producing entirely new fibres for her knitwear. Many of the materials she now incorporates into her knits have no place otherwise in fashion but come from developments such as the emergence of the fibre optics industry. In this preparatory work, her scientific training has obviously been of great assistance but so too has the possession of an abundant imagination, allowing her to see

RIGHT **One of Lainey Keogh's earliest champions was singer Marianne Faithfull, photographed in 1991 in the Shell Cottage at Carton, Co Kildare. Faithfull, who modelled for the designer during London Fashion Week in September 1997, says that Keogh's clothes "are both sexy and sensual, very elegant and easy to wear. They have got this subtle sexuality which I like."**

BELOW **Lainey Keogh's debt to Ireland's traditional knitwear is very evident. This white cotton bobble-knit top from her spring/summer 1988 collection makes no secret of its inspiration, but already Keogh is beginning to play with both form and surface to create a garment with its own distinctive identity.**

the possibilities in yarns which no other designer would consider. "In a way, fibre comes before form," she told the *Financial Times* in September 1997. "Each collection starts with a yarn. We begin with a tiny fibre, we create our own textiles and then we translate each into its own unique language, a finished knit which has both form and meaning."

By the time she presented her third collection at the London Fashion Week of February 1998, Lainey Keogh was being hailed by *The Times* as "Ireland's spinner of dreams" and a designer, according to *The Guardian* "clearly not limited by traditional notions of knitwear". Nonetheless, the sense of tradition has remained subtly evident in her work. The *International Herald Tribune's* influential fashion editor Suzy Menkes said of Lainey Keogh in 1998 that "she does seem to capture the spirit of Ireland in her knitting without being obvious. People are looking for modern romance – we've all had it with minimalism – and she provides a very modern way of having romantic clothes." Romanticism has always been a feature of the designer's clothes, along with a powerful element of sensuality. "Lainey's success is based on the fact that she understands women," explains Andrew Tucker. "Unlike a lot of designers who don't understand sex very well, her work is very much about sexuality. She always talks about the feel factor in her garments and everything has to be voluptuous and incredibly comfortable. I think a lot of female designers are scared of that approach whereas Lainey embraces it. She's the Irish designer I admire most because a lot of her work is quite radical and yet it has this inherent luxury too."

Luxuriantly sensual but designed for the strong-minded, independent woman, using technologically advanced fibres but made by the ancient means of hand-knitting – these are some of the contradictions which Lainey Keogh's clothes have managed to reconcile with apparent effortlessness. "Lainey's work has dovetailed with two big trends in fashion in the 1990s," Godfrey Deeny comments. "It has a unique mixture of the artisanal which is now very popular, but it also uses new technology in the yarns which are spun for her." In addition, she has thrown into the mix her very powerful eye for colour – which again might be considered distinctively Irish – and an awareness not shared by many other designers of the female body in all its voluptuous grace. "My work

This heavy cotton man's sweater dating from autumn/winter 1989 was called "Newgrange" and reflects Lainey Keogh's abiding interest in Ireland's past. For some years she produced a succession of collections in which patterns taken from ancient Irish stone carvings and illustrated manuscripts were used.

is sculptural, the body dictates the form of my garments. Not the other way around," she told the *Irish Times* in April 1994. "This is the reality of working with fibre rather than cloth." But she has freed fibre from its own constrictions and eloquently demonstrated that in knitwear today almost anything is feasible.

Young knitwear designers

Lainey Keogh's innovations have been to the advantage of a younger generation of knitwear designers, not least Liam Grier who, at the age of 24, won first prize at the Taispeántas na Sionainne fashion show in Athlone in October 1997. Originally from Ramelton, County Donegal and still a student at the Limerick School of Art and Design when he won this award, he creates knits which have a sensuality similar to that of Lainey Keogh. Another shared feature is his interest in new fibre technology; in one of his first collections, he used a synthetic yarn called ilaira which gives clothes additional stretch and cling. Liam Grier also likes to give his designs strong surface interest, with elaborate patterns and textures woven into each knit. While there are no obvious connections with the traditional Aran sweater, perhaps this abiding concern with creating a sense of movement in the garment indicates a traceable lineage in Irish knitwear.

The same feature is apparent too in the work of Elaine Curtis, another young knitter who won the Taispeántas an Sionainne award the year before Liam Grier. Born in Carlow, from where she now runs her business, she attended Limerick School of Art and Design before beginning to work on her own in late 1997. Her designs, like those of other Irish knitwear producers who emerged in the 1990s, are far more overtly sensual than used to be the case and are worked in jewel-rich colours. While the shapes are uncomplicated, once more the advantages of contemporary technology permit elaborate surface texture.

As the twentieth century ended, interest in knitwear had been renewed and revitalised in Ireland. The three winners in the 1999 Smirnoff student fashion awards, for example, all produced knitted collections (and all of them had come out of the Limerick School of Art and Design). It therefore seems likely that the country's close association with knitwear will remain strong for some time to come.

Lainey Keogh wears her own work to perfection. It often seems as though no shape, no colour does not suit her. As is indicated here by the fur collar on her dress, she also relishes her sense of touch and says that her clothes are "all about feel appeal". This is why so many women love to wear her knits; they possess an inherent quality of indulgence.

Although Ireland experienced an economic boom during the final decade of the twentieth century, many of the country's finest young designers continued to move and work elsewhere. Why should this have been so? At last there was enough money around to support youthful talent and, in addition, abundant creativity seemed to be found in every artistic discipline. But no matter how wealthy, Ireland's population is never going to be able to sustain a large fashion industry. Even the most successful names in the business continue to rely heavily on exports – and on presenting their clothes at overseas shows and fairs - in order to continue working at home. Ireland now annually produces more fashion graduates than she can provide with jobs; with up to fifty new designers emerging from Irish colleges each summer, some of them have to leave so that others can stay at home.

It would be wrong to suggest that Ireland's fashion diaspora is necessarily a misfortune. There are great advantages in going abroad, at least for a period, in order to acquire expertise in one of the world's great fashion capitals. Major centres such as London, Paris, Milan and New York offer opportunities which could never be found in Dublin, not least the chance to work in a long-established house. "The one piece of advice I've always given to students is to go abroad," Michael Mortell says. "Work in that atmosphere for a number of years. Whether it's a French or an Italian company, these are very powerful big houses and they will have built in great business systems. See how the ranges are produced, bathe yourself in that professionalism for a number of years and then, if you want to, come back and set up a business here." Cities such as Milan or Paris enjoy the benefits of a culture more sympathetic to the specific requirements of fashion, as well as providing the very best facilities. Many commentators point out, for example, that the Milanese fashion industry can always depend on receiving plenty of support from Italian fabric manufacturers who recognise their own success is built on that of major labels such as Armani and Versace.

"The best career advice I could give to a young designer is to get out of Ireland for five or ten years," is also Godfrey Deeny's recommendation. "Then return if you wish. In the late 1970s, Irish design graduates began to move to places like Paris and Milan where they could gain a great deal of experience and a small reputation. And that's the true finishing school of fashion. If you look at the history of the industry, this has always been the case. Designers have served their ten or fifteen years of apprenticeship in existing houses and only become famous in their late thirties or forties. This sort of thing doesn't happen overnight, it takes a couple of decades, but we're beginning to see the fruits of that experience."

Philip Treacy

Of course, not every designer who leaves the country is going to come back again and a feature of the 1990s was the emergence of a generation of designers globally recognised as Irish even though they were not based in Ireland. The best-known of these and certainly the most famous Irish designer in the world today is milliner Philip Treacy. It is impossible to find anyone associated with the fashion business capable of speaking ill of this designer. Hamish Bowles, for example, enthuses about his play of proportion, sense of scale and methods of fabrication, remarking how Philip Treacy "has taken a division of the apparel industry which had become rather moribund and turned it into something exciting. His hats are all about incredible precision of construction and a really dramatic sense of craftsmanship. He's really a designer who pushes fashion forward even though he's not producing clothing." Similarly, Paula Reed says: "Philip is a huge favourite of mine and one of the most exciting talents ever to come out of Ireland. His work goes beyond millinery. He made a headdress for my wedding where he took the most unprepossessing material, taking some filaments of something almost like fishing wire and then threading this with little bits of lily of the valley silk flowers to make this confection. To this day, I don't know how he did it."

Like so many other Irish designers, Philip Treacy's origins hardly seem conducive to an international career in fashion. Born in 1967, he grew up in Ahascragh, a small town in County Galway. "When I was about six or seven," he explains, "I asked my teacher Mrs McDonagh why the boys didn't sew while the girls did and could I learn to do it. She was a bit taken aback, but she taught me. By the time I left school, she had all the boys sewing, knitting and crocheting – although I couldn't really knit." One of eight children, he seems to have had an extremely happy childhood in which his fashion interests were supported by his family. "As a child, I loved to make things – toys, Christmas decorations, clothes. I remember once somebody remarking to my father 'Don't you think it's a bit strange?' when I was making clothes for my sister's dolls. And my father said, 'whatever makes him happy' which is the most wonderful reply from someone who wasn't surrounded by design or art."

On leaving school, Philip Treacy went first to Galway Regional Technical College for a year and then to Dublin where he studied fashion at the National College of Art and Design. It seems clear that his sights were set on moving abroad even then. "When I was a student in Dublin in the mid-1980s, it didn't seem Irish fashion had a contemporary feel to it. It felt separate to what was going on in the rest of the world. As students we slightly felt we were missing out on something. But in fact, when I came to London, I realised that not having had the same influences as everyone else, I'd had to find my own ones." In 1988, Philip Treacy won a scholarship to London's Royal College of Art and ever since has been based in the English capital, where he has had his own premises on Elizabeth Street since 1991.

Even as a student, he was working with other designers such as John Galliano and Rifat Ozbek and in the 1990s, he began a long-standing professional relationship with Chanel and its designer Karl Lagerfeld, as well as Valentino and Versace. Although he produces two collections annually, he stages his own show once a year. "From working with Lagerfeld I learnt about the power of a hat on the runway," he says. "I remember the first time I worked with him. I'd never used the big international models before and there was a fantastic moment when Linda Evangelista was going out wearing one of my hats. She waited until all the other girls were off the runway before making her entrance. That was a very important moment because suddenly I saw this thing I'd made on one of the most important models in the world."

As many observers have noted, what marks Philip Treacy apart is not just his creativity but the fact that he has chosen to exercise this in the specialist field of millinery. His interest in hats began while he was still a student in Dublin, where he would make items to accompany the clothes he had designed. "There came a time when I enjoyed making the hats more than the clothes. When I started in the 'eighties, they were beginning to have an old-fashioned association. But I've always designed hats as though they've never disappeared from fashion. My obsession with modernity in hat-making has carried me along. Also I think accessories used to be a slight complement to fashion. But fashion has become very expensive so now hats, bags and things like that are a relatively inexpensive way of making something very simple look better." Philip Treacy's hats are frequently so dramatic that they work best when worn with the simplest items of clothing, thereby avoiding the risk of visual confrontation.

In his work, he is as much an engineer as a designer, since he has to resolve technical difficulties involving not just unusual materials but also highly unorthodox shapes that must sit comfortably on the wearer's head. Recent collections have included large metallic saucers perched in front of the face as well as fibre-optic neon strands shooting out from a central base. His show in February 1999 featured a hat designed to emulate a turreted gothic castle and another looking like one of American artist Alexander Calder's mobile sculptures. Since 1997, he has also produced an associated range of handbags, gloves, scarves and hair pieces, while also designing an inexpensive range of hats for the Debenham's department store chain. "Because I come from a background that wasn't moneyed," he says, "I am concerned with value for money. When I started working at that price point, there was a feeling the customer wouldn't understand. But the customer is very discerning and becoming more so all the time so I think it's important to be able to sell at every level." It is an indication of this designer's supremacy in his chosen field that since 1991, he has been awarded the title of British Accessory Designer of the Year no less than five times.

Understandably, Philip Treacy is often not considered Irish by outside observers. "For me Philip is an international designer. I think his Irishness is incidental and he could operate out of New York or London or Paris," comments Hamish Bowles, although he does concede that "although he avoids the folkloric route, he does draw on the tradition of craft and attention to detail which is Irish." Paula Reed, on the other hand, believes the designer "has a very lyrical, romantic sense of shape and colour and style. That lyricism and romance absolutely comes from his Irish background." Perhaps

Philip Treacy's Irishness is expressed in a more subliminal manner than that of other designers, but he himself believes it can be found in his work. "Where I came from bore very little relevance to the world of design," he explains. "But in fact it's where I get my favourite inspiration from because I grew up in the countryside and I was surrounded by beautiful things always. For many years I didn't find a connection between what I did and where I came from, but it was really very obvious and just took me a long time to realise that. My work is influenced by nature itself and by natural, fluid lines."

Slim Barrett

"I've always promoted myself as Irish because I've never seen any reason not to do so," remarks Philip Treacy. The same might be said of two other Irish designers who, like him, have Galway origins and specialise in accessories. Jeweller Slim Barrett was born in Athenry in 1960 and originally trained as a sculptor in Galway. He moved to London in the mid-1980s and has been based there ever since. What distinguishes his work are precisely those qualities which are so frequently assigned to Irish designers: a lyrical romanticism and a love of fine craft. During the early part of his career, the pieces he produced were frequently baroque in character and included silver chainmail torsos, belts studded with glass bullets and enormous pendular earrings hung with pearls. However, during the 1990s, he was inclined to create jewellery of steadily finer proportions such as the whimsically dainty gothic tiaras that he was largely responsible for making fashionable, especially among brides, and that were described by the *Guardian* as being "the stuff a modernday Titania's dreams are made of". When Spice Girl Victoria Adams married David Beckham at Luttrellstown Castle in July 1999, she wore a Slim Barrett eighteen-carat gold coronet incorporating more than one hundred and fifty diamonds. At the same time, the designer won the De Beers Diamonds-International Award for a necklace he had made using over ninety-five carats of diamonds and worth more than £1 million. Like Philip Treacy, Slim Barrett has collaborated with many fashion designers including Lagerfeld, Versace, Montana and Ungaro.

Olivia Morris

Shoe designer Olivia Morris is considerably younger than Slim Barrett but she too has already begun working with designers such as London's Anthony Symonds, for whom she produced a range of footwear seen at his show in February 1998. Although much of her childhood was spent in England, she spent summer holidays in County Galway – her grandfather was the late Lord Killanin, former chairman of the International Olympics Committee – and perceives herself to be Irish. Today, she is based in London, having attended the city's Cordwainers College which specialises in training shoe designers; regrettably, no such specialist studies are available in Ireland. In September 1999, she opened her own small outlet on the Portobello Road carrying a full range of shoes and bags. The latter range, called Slag Bags, are noteworthy for their wit, a rare quality in fashion. Small clutches, for example, come with metal studded wristbands or even a single handcuff. Studding also featured on her range of shoes for autumn/winter 1999 where it appeared on boxy square heels designed to emulate old-fashioned trunk luggage. Speaking of her work, Olivia Morris remarks, "I would definitely say there is an element of tradition left in Irish fashion. After all, making shoes is a very traditional business. I'd imagine that's also true for people like John Rocha and Lainey Keogh. Even if they're designing something modern, the basis of their work – and mine – lies in tradition and traditional techniques."

Daryl Kerrigan

London has long held a powerful allure for Irish designers. In the 1990s, however, other cities began to look just as attractive. One of these was New York, centre of the powerful American fashion industry. The sheer scale of that industry would suggest that a new young designer without connections could not hope to become successful, but the career of Daryl Kerrigan proves otherwise. A Dubliner, she attended the National College of Art and Design (where she was a year ahead of Philip Treacy) and after graduating in 1986 immediately moved to the United States. "I used to come to New York in the summers when I was a student," is how she explains this decision to leave Ireland. However, finding employment in Manhattan was not easy. "I couldn't get a job in design even after I graduated, so I worked as a waitress for a year. Then I quit and got work in the movie business." Initially, she was employed as a wardrobe assistant for $125 a week but gradually she began to establish her reputation in the film business. The last project on which she worked as a costume designer was "My Cousin Vinny", released in 1992. By then, she had left film and opened her own shop. There are a number of reasons why she chose to change direction just as her prospects began to improve: "Well, in the movie business you can't be that creative. There are so many things like the director, the actors, the writer, the setting. It's fascinating and I loved it but everything I wanted to do, it was 'no, no, no'."

Daryl Kerrigan's success in the United States was remarkably fast. In February 1997, she was awarded the Perry Ellis Award for Young Designer of the Year by the Council of Fashion Designers in America and her reputation as a new star was confirmed. Back in her native country almost no one knew of her work, which was not being stocked by any Irish retailers. "I really think a few of my clothes should be in Dublin," she drily observed. There can be no doubt that Daryl Kerrigan's rise in the United States was due as much to her being in the right place at the right time as to her indisputable talent. Andrew Tucker was one of the first journalists on this side of the Atlantic to spot her potential and he comments, "Daryl Kerrigan has a strong urban sportswear sensibility which really hadn't existed in the American milieu before. She brought a real freshness to the scene. Her designs were quite radical in the context of American fashion which is extremely market-driven and quite bland actually. Going to a Daryl Kerrigan show in New York, there's a buzz which is very cutting-edge for America."

The designer established her cutting-edge credentials from the start by taking premises on East Sixth Street in SoHo, an area of Manhattan which then had few fashion outlets but has since become heavily colonised by the best-known names in the industry. With no experience in the business, Daryl Kerrigan quickly learnt about the pitfalls of retailing. When she opened her shop in late summer 1991, "There were two machines in the back and I used to make all the clothes myself. The bell would ring and I'd run out and sell, doing all the fittings. Right away, I was cracking up, laughing with nervousness. There's a strangeness in someone giving you money if you've never been a merchant."

The inherent conservatism of American fashion meant that her clothes with their urban sensibility immediately stood out and were noticed. "She did something very significant," Godfrey Deeny explains. "She really connected with lots of young editors and stylists on important fashion magazines and they wore lots of her clothes. These are frequently the most advantageous people to dress – not actresses or models or rock stars – because once you have them as an audience, you're almost assured of success." Daryl Kerrigan's name, along with her work, soon began to feature in American style magazines and by the mid-1990s her label, called Daryl K, had become synonymous with hip young urban style.

Japan, a country always keenly interested in new western fashion trends, also quickly caught on to Daryl Kerrigan. Her first wholesale importer was Japanese and outside the United States, Japan remains her biggest market. Today, she is stocked by every major American department store and has two outlets, having opened a second on Bond Street in Manhattan in 1996. At the same time, she also added another line to her range; called K-189, this is less expensive than the main collection.

Her first signature piece was the bootleg hipster pants which went on to become a favourite item of the decade. "A lot of people think they were responsible for the bootleg hipster," she said in 1996, "but I know we did it first. Our cut and pattern have been taken by other people; that's how fashion works and there's nothing you can do about it."

While the urban environment still appears to provide her primary source of inspiration, commercial success has allowed Daryl Kerrigan gradually to create work more elaborate in both design and manufacture. Instead of making the clothes up herself in a backroom, she now has many of them produced in Italy. "That's the pay-off for getting to a higher level," she explains, remarking of the Italian companies she uses, "The way things are made is really refined." As for her more technically complex designs, she says "I think the clothes are getting more sophisticated but I don't believe they're losing any of their original spirit." Typical of the sophisticated yet sporty pieces from her autumn/winter 1999 collection was a black wool skirt with tabard front and back held in place by four buckles on either side, and what she called her "chill-chaser jacket" in quilted steel-fibred nylon, a fabric originally made for lining space craft. This interest in technologically advanced materials she shares with Lainey Keogh but whereas the latter uses new fibres to produce deeply romantic clothes, those designed by Daryl Kerrigan are quite clearly intended to convey the wearer's street-wise savvy. Because of this, it is hard to find any elements in her work which mark this designer out as overtly Irish.

While she regularly returns to Dublin, where her clothes finally found an outlet in autumn 1999, the public perception of Daryl Kerrigan is of someone with a decisively American approach to fashion. "I don't think of Daryl as Irish," agrees Hamish Bowles. "I think of her absolutely as being an East Village girl with a dream and a sewing machine who has the ability to capture the spirit of downtown. She has taken a lot of elements of sports clothing – be it velcro fastenings or sweatpants -and adapted them into pieces you can wear on the street or in a nightclub. She tends to deconstruct clothes and put zips or pockets in unexpected places. She's providing hip, easy clothes that are statement-y without being bizarre." Indisputably her profile has been helped by doing this work in New York rather than, for example, London where the connection between innovation on the street and in high fashion is far more common. But as Hamish Bowles says, "Daryl would have been a success wherever she set up because she has a sensibility and a vision that sets her apart from the common herd."

Sharon Wauchob

This is true also of another Irish designer who chose to settle away from home in the 1990s. Sharon Wauchob only staged her first show in March 1998 but already she had been noticed by influential fashion editors and buyers; her final show of the decade was notable for the number of Japanese retailers present – always a good endorsement for a young designer. Born in County Tyrone in 1971, she grew up an only child on a farm and says that as a child, "I wasn't thinking of fashion in the commercial sense but more in the artistic. I spent a lot of time drawing and later that progressed into fashion. I was aware that a lot of the clothes I saw seemed to me to be getting it wrong and I kept hooking things up the side and playing with clothes in the changing room, probably irritating my mother quite a lot. Later on, I began to see some of what I was thinking was maybe happening elsewhere at the time." After thinking she might take over the family farm, at nineteen she went to study fashion at St Martin's College in London. The day after she qualified, the Japanese designer Koji Tatsuno telephoned her offering a job with him; she took it and stayed for the next four years. She has subsequently worked for Louis Vuitton, the French luxury goods company.

While she shares with this brand an interest in creating products of the highest possible quality, her work shows clearer affinities with her first employer. Much admired by the fashion press, Koji Tatsuno is barely known to the general public. He has a special interest in the possibilities of unusual materials in clothing and usually produces small collections of very elaborately constructed garments. In addition, like many of his fellow countrymen, he does not feel constricted by tradition in form. When the school of Japanese designers first came to prominence in Europe during the 1980s, what particularly marked them apart – aside from a propensity to use black – was a refusal to insist that any item of clothing ought to take cognisance of the body beneath.

This is also often true of Sharon Wauchob's designs, which can take on the character of wearable sculpture. It is significant that she speaks of "constructing" rather than designing a collection. Her clothes, like those of the Japanese and Belgian designers she particularly admires, display a constant curiosity about fabric's possibilities and involve much gathering, folding and wrapping as well as elaborate pleating and stitching techniques. She has found a ready market for her work in Japan – "I just seemed to get a reaction there and I used it" – but she has also started to export elsewhere around the world. International sales have been helped by staging shows in Paris and while she admits that the familiar format of models walking by an audience might be considered rather old-fashioned, "my clothes work best when they're on women; there's a feeling of reality and movement. The show gives an understanding of my clothes. A lot of them, if they're on a hanger people don't know which is the front and which the back. So unless they have a booklet to explain it, there are going to be problems." Shows also attract press attention and one result of those organised by Sharon Wauchob has been coverage in many fashion magazines such as *Vogue*, *The Face* and *I.D.*

What has most caught media attention is her fresh approach to the material with which she works. "I quite like taking fabrics out of context," she told the *Irish Times* in June 1998, "like making a silk chiffon jacket which gives a hint of surprise. And I'd rather hide some elements, for example mohair peeking through chiffon." While her debut collection was defined by its uncompromisingly bold structures, her fourth – for spring/summer 2000 – was, she confirms, softer in spirit and possessing a greater sense of femininity than hitherto. She suggests this reflects her Irish origins, as does her sense of light and tone in clothing. "The strongest part in me identifiable with Ireland is colour and the way I use it. I can use forty shades of grey and think they're different colours. When you look at the light in Ireland, I think you can see the link with that."

Nonetheless, she believes it is to her own advantage to leave Ireland. "I think you have to travel. Fashion is becoming more and more international and you have to be nomadic. Your market is not located in any one country so you have to be aware of what's happening elsewhere." The experience of Sharon Wauchob and her peers showed that in the 1990s, it was possible to achieve success as an Irish designer – and be recognised as such – without remaining in Ireland. The fashion diaspora had reached maturity.

RIGHT **This photograph shows Marc O'Neill in a more romantic mood than usual, and permits him to demonstrate a greater degree of technical wizardry in the way the white cotton shirt has been caught and gathered under the bust. Notice too how the trousers have been permitted to expose seams normally concealed inside.**

In the second half of the 1990s, Ireland experienced an economic boom which seems to have caught many of the country's inhabitants by surprise, so accustomed had they become to retrenchment and recession. Throughout the decade, the average annual GNP was close to six per cent and was predicted to stay at five per cent into the new millennium. Better times really had arrived – for fashion as much as any other sector - and they quickly started to make an impact. In 1994, for example, the Irish Trade Board produced a report called *Market Opportunities in Ireland for Clothing*. This noted that annual sales of women's clothes in the country were now worth £660 million and rising. The reasons given for this rise included a growth of twenty-one per cent in disposable income during the preceding four years, and an increase of more than fifteen per cent in the 25-44 age category between 1981 and 1991. The same report also remarked that consumers had become more fashion-conscious than before and naturally this could be seen as beneficial to the country's clothing industry although, as was to become apparent, companies still not able to adapt to changing circumstances would remain vulnerable. Another feature of the 1990s was the radical drop in the country's unemployment figures. By 1999, thanks to the creation of more than 350,000 new jobs over the previous five years, a record 1.5 million people were employed within the Republic. The outcome was a severe labour shortage; it now became customary for shops, restaurants and other members of the service industry to search without success for sufficient staff. Even though the size of the clothing industry was smaller than ever before, employers here too were no longer able to recruit qualified machinists or pattern cutters.

By January 1999, annual inflation had dropped to 1.5 per cent and emigration rates also tumbled, replaced instead by large numbers of Irish nationals returning to work at home. The Central Statistics Office observed that in the year ended April 1998, net immigrations reached a historical highpoint of 22,800.

Among those who chose to return to Ireland in the 1990s was Dubliner Melanie Morris who, having worked in public relations in London for a number of years, started a new publication in 1992 called *D'Side*. If *I.T.* and *Image* had done much to help promote Irish fashion during the 1970s and 1980s, *D'Side* performed the same function during the last decade of the century. A youth style magazine, it consistently championed new young talents and proposed that what was being produced in Ireland was as good as that found anywhere else. "When we started, there was nothing else like it in the country," Melanie Morris remembers. "Independent publishing was beginning to emerge all over the world with titles like *Dazed and Confused* and *Scene*. So we felt the youth market was now big enough to sustain a magazine here."

Ireland's economic and demographic expansions were met by a corresponding explosion in retail. Every large city and town acquired large new shopping centres and these quickly came to do record business. In 1995/1996, for example, the greater Dublin area acquired an extra one million square feet of retail space and, over the next few years, this amount was increased by an additional 1.5 million square feet thanks to the arrival of shopping centres such as Liffey Valley; even though this had 250,000 square feet of space, within less than six months of its opening in October 1998, plans had been drawn up for the centre to double in size. A typical instance of the capital's retail resurgence was the £45 million refurbishment of Arnott's which, beginning in 1996, saw this department store expand from 165,000 to 295,000 square feet. Although the capital and its suburbs accounted for more than thirty per cent of retail turnover in the country, such growth was not confined to Dublin. In March 1998, the Brown Thomas group reopened its department store in Cork after a £12 million-plus overhaul which saw the interior space grow from 45,000 to 75,000 square feet.

Naturally, all these new shops attracted plenty of high-spending consumers. In December 1997, the Central Statistics Office released figures showing that retail sales during the previous three years had risen by 28 per cent. However, Irish companies were not necessarily the beneficiaries of this development in consumerism. At the start of the decade, total spending on clothes in Ireland was estimated to be in the region of £950 million, but imports accounted for almost four-fifths of that figure, with half of them coming from Britain. Attempting to fight against this tide of imports, in 1990 Coras Tráchtála joined forces with twenty-one Irish clothing companies to start a "Look to our Own" campaign intended to encourage the public to buy domestically-produced goods. Two years later, "Look to our Own" became more specific, focusing on individual brand names and ranges. But it was a struggle which could never hope for more than limited success.

As Ireland became richer, the country seemed ever more enticing to British clothing manufacturers and retailers who, finding their home market saturated and stagnant, turned to an immediate neighbour for expansionist opportunities. And for many of them this proved to be a smart move; in January 1999, the manager of Marks & Spencer in Ireland told the *Irish Times* that the company's fastest sales growth during the preceding three years had been seen in its Irish outlets. Ireland had always seen Britain as the most convenient market for its goods. Now that situation was reversed and in the 1990s many Irish towns came to see their principal streets dominated by names such as Next, Laura Ashley, Oasis and Miss Selfridge. Irish retailers found themselves unable to compete since they were not part of large, multi-national companies backed by substantial revenues. The British chains were often preferred by developers of Ireland's new shopping centres, since they were perceived to be more reliable than local groups and able to pay larger rents.

The result was an increasing homogeneity in Irish retailing of a kind already familiar to British shoppers. Most commercial developments, no matter where their location around the country, featured the same well-known brands, and a loss of local identity was the detrimental outcome. But a further consequence of the British multiples' arrival in Ireland was the continuing decline of Irish clothing manufacturers. Local companies could not hope to match the cheap prices charged for their goods by chains who had switched manufacturing to countries where labour costs were low, notably south-east Asia and north Africa. The most competitive Irish retailers understandably followed suit, and groups like Dunnes Stores began to carry large quantities of clothing made outside Ireland. Manufacturers at home were left without any support, and many of them closed. In Donegal, the American-owned Fruit of the Loom clothing company, which at its height had employed around 3,000 people, announced almost 800 redundancies in December 1998 when it was decided to transfer T-shirt sewing operations to Morocco.

Nine months later, the Dublin clothing company J.A. Hickey, in business since 1965, finally closed with the loss of one hundred and seventy jobs. In a statement released at the time, managing director John Hickey said the company had "reluctantly concluded that trading conditions will only disimprove. For some time the company has found it increasingly difficult to compete with manufacturers in south-east Asia, north Africa and the Baltic States." Hickey's was essentially a mass-market clothing producer but its problems were not so very different from those faced by companies making quality goods. In autumn 1999, citing "unprecedented challenges," the Irish Clothing Manufacturers' Federation announced that "the traditional focus on manufacturing activities is no longer the key to success."

From Marc O'Neill's first collection for A Wear in autumn/winter 1995, this bomber jacket is made in fake crocodile skin, showing the designer's particular skill as a tailor combined with an ability to use unusual fabrics. O'Neill has never been too much of a showman, however, as seen by the way he combines the jacket with a classic pair of chalkstripe trousers.

Around the same time, the Economic and Social Research Institute released figures to show that the clothing business in Ireland, having employed some 20,000 people in 1981, could only sustain 12,000 jobs by 1995 and would have no more than 9,000 of these in the year 2003. It was a sign of the times when in mid-October 1999 John Rocha announced his intention to sign a licensing agreement with a Portuguese company which would assume responsibility for all his clothing manufacture and distribution.

Jen Kelly

While Rocha continued to expand, other designers were not so fortunate. After Ib Jorgensen closed his house in 1994, only a handful of couturiers remained in business, most notably Thomas Wolfangel and Pat Crowley. The solitary newcomer in this division of fashion was Derry-born Jen Kelly. He had studied both marketing and design, undoubtedly one reason why since 1989 he had been able to maintain a couture house, albeit on a much smaller scale than his predecessors. His business in Dublin depends on a relatively modest number of clients who wish to buy clothes made especially for them, usually for specific events such as weddings or charity balls. But while he may be based in Ireland, his sensibility – like that of his clientele – is essentially international, the fabrics he uses come mostly from Italian houses and the designs he offers reflect those worn by affluent French or German women.

Mariad Whisker

One of the great losses to Ireland's fashion business was the departure of Mariad Whisker. Born in Belfast, she studied at Manchester Art College before taking a job as a knitwear designer for small Irish companies, followed by a spell working in London. In 1981, she returned to Ireland and set up her own label in Dublin, initially selling work at the Design Centre. Her fluid, layered clothes tended to display the influence of Japanese fashion as filtered through an Irish sensibility and they enjoyed a considerable vogue. In 1993, she won the Late, Late Show Designer of the Year award, but within twelve months announced her intention to leave Ireland and move to the United States with her family. In an interview with the *Irish Times* before her departure, she explained that the combination of high tax and low salaries was among the reasons behind her decision. In addition, she said, "Design just doesn't have the respect that it has in other countries. We are treated like the lowest form of industry yet the fashion business is a labour-intensive one." Mariad Whisker's work has been intermittently available in Ireland since she left and continues to cause a stir whenever it is shown. Like many designers, she faced the problem of having to run a small business even though her primary interest lay in creating clothes – "At the moment, I am designer, cutter and everything else," she told the *Irish Times* in September 1994. Her story was by no means unusual, and helps to explain why so few young Irish designers take the risk of starting their own label; working for an established house guarantees security.

But it would be wrong to conclude that Ireland's fashion industry was facing extinction during a decade in which so many other businesses blossomed. As always, it was the companies which adapted best to altered circumstances that enjoyed economic growth. In April 1999, the Clubman Omega shirt company opened new premises in Buncrana, Co Donegal. In the mid-1980s, the company had twice gone into receivership and when new management took over in 1986, its annual turnover was in the region of £800,000. By the end of the 1990s, that figure had grown to almost £4 million and was climbing at a yearly rate of twenty per cent. As managing director Sean Tighe explained to the *Irish Times*, Clubman could not hope to compete with low-cost imports and therefore concentrated on carving out its own place in the middle-to-upper end of the market. This was where the future of Ireland's surviving clothing industry lay. Clubman not only produced its own-label shirts but in addition 25 per cent of its business lay in manufacturing garments for such designers as John Rocha, Paul Costelloe and Paul Smith.

It was at this end of the market too that growth was seen in exports during the 1990s. Even if the number of jobs in the industry went down, the total value of Irish clothing steadily rose. By 1998 annual sales of Irish garments overseas had reached almost £350 million, of which Britain (including Northern Ireland) accounted for approximately fifty per cent. There were drawbacks for such heavy dependence on one market; in July 1994, for example, the *Irish Times* reported that clothing firms were concerned with the strength of the Irish pound against sterling. However, for much of the decade, the latter currency was the more powerful and this could only benefit exporters of Irish goods. Andrew Tucker, who has advised a number of Irish clothing companies how to develop their British market, comments "Lots of people love the product coming from Ireland which isn't high fashion. It's middle market, good quality and with enough fashion awareness to make it exciting. It's for a woman who's not fashion-obsessed but doesn't want to look frumpy. What's interesting about these Irish labels is that five or six years ago, stores in Britain buying at that level were going to Germany and now they're looking to Ireland which is slightly more fashion aware." Of course, this close association with Britain has meant that other countries in Europe were left almost untapped. Enterprise Ireland's Jim Maguire confirms that for the majority of Irish clothing manufacturers, Britain remains the only export goal. "European markets tend to be different in terms of sizing, colour ways and even fabrics," he says. "But there's also a problem of perception. Mainland Europe tends to be seen as harder because places like Paris and Milan are fashion centres and so harder to break into. People are less confident about selling here although there are opportunities."

Marc O'Neill

Indeed, 1990 - 2000 was a decade of opportunities but only a handful of young designers appeared to be prepared to take advantage of them. The most successful of these was Dubliner Marc O'Neill who, while still a student at the National College of Art and Design, had been spotted by experienced players in the fashion industry as a talent to watch. No wonder, therefore, that in 1995, having spent a year away from Ireland studying design management at university in Leicester, aged only 24, he was given a chance to produce a range of garments for the A Wear chain. "It was quite hard to convince the company I was capable of doing the work," he now says. "I suggested that if I put together a small capsule collection, we would try it out. The hard side for me was confronting the whole manufacturing side of things. When you work on a mainstream collection that's going to be mass-produced and worn by thousands of people, not just a small group of fashion followers, it has to work and technically it has be very good." Fortunately his first range, in which fluid jersey pieces predominated, did work and he has remained associated with A Wear ever since, while also designing his own, more expensive range. His large number of private clients such as The Corrs has allowed Marc O'Neill the chance to refine key skills. "Working on a couture basis," he commented in the mid-1990s, "you learn a lot about the body and good fit. In the mass market, you're working all the time on size specifications that have been around for years and you don't tend to keep in touch with your customer base."

Marc O'Neill's skill lies in creating pared-back clothing which is youthful in spirit but not excessively concerned with acknowledging every passing fashion trend. He sums up his work as being "quirky contemporary tailoring for the self-assured". In this respect, he represents a continuation of Ireland's long-established tradition of tailoring and shares Louise Kennedy's interest in beautiful, understated work. The designers he most admires, like Germany's Jil Sander and the Austrian Helmut Lang, like clean cutting and use of the finest possible fabrics and these qualities may be discerned in his own work also. He described his designs to *Elle* magazine in October 1997 as "simple and refined. They're for people who like sharp cut without fussy detail." He once explained this preference for simplicity by remarking "I don't think anyone should be weighed down by clothes." Now barely thirty, he is much more focused and ambitious than most Irish designers of his generation and he has a keen awareness of what his customers – professional urban women of his own age group – require. "I think Marc O'Neill has added a nice urban twist to Irish fashion," comments *D'Side's* Melanie Morris. "His clothes can hang just as well in New York or London shops as in Irish ones. They're young and punchy but not gimmicky. They'll last longer than the season

When Cuan Hanly was invited to design a menswear collection for the A Wear group in September 1996, his brief was to produce a stylish range which would not alienate existing clients by having too many fussy details. As shown by this suit from his autumn/winter 1998, he managed to do just what was asked of him, at a reasonable price.

they're designed for because they've got more substance to them. They're very easy to wear and they don't involve dressing up."

Working with A Wear over five years has only heightened Marc O'Neill's inherent awareness of the marketplace and its demands. "It has certainly given me a lot of commercial sense," he told the *Irish Times* in 1996, adding that the chainstore's bosses had advised him "to design not just with my creative mind but with my retailing mind as well." He points out that working for a chainstore, "you can't use very expensive fabrics and there's only so much detail you can put into a garment without it becoming too lengthy to make

timewise because obviously that's a cost factor. But while that's a compromise, it's also a great challenge. I think when you've a big budget behind you, it's very easy to be creative; when you've got restrictions, it presents a challenge I really enjoy." In September 1999, he held his first solo show during London Fashion Week in an East End warehouse and has been steadily developing his export business; his clothes are already stocked by both Saks and Barney's department stores in New York.

Cuan Hanly

Perhaps because his family background was in the clothing business, Marc O'Neill has a more acute sense of commerce than is usually found among fashion designers. However, this understanding is shared by another name who emerged in the 1990s, Cuan Hanly. He is also unusual in choosing to specialise in menswear, a sector which has never been particularly well-served in Ireland. "When I was at college in the mid-1980s," he explains, "men's fashion in Ireland wasn't particularly up to much, which begs the question why I ever went into it. But I did feel there was potential growth in the market and that has now started." A number of the country's designers, such as John Rocha and Paul Costelloe, do produce lines of clothing for men, but this is not the area in which they began their careers and made their names. Cuan Hanly's only obvious predecessor in this field was Nicky Wallace, who had a glorious but brief career during the 1980s when his annual turnover at one stage reached close to £1 million. From a long-established men's tailoring business in Wexford, he was so successful that his suits were worn by actor Don Johnson in the television series "Miami Vice". But over-ambitious expansion led to collapse and while he returned to business in the mid-1990s, Nicky Wallace never managed to repeat the previous decade's success.

Cuan Hanly, on the other hand, looks set for steady growth thanks, in part at least, to a very finely-tuned understanding of his market. "I think it's invaluable for a designer to know about the business aspect," he said when first setting up his own company. "Even if you've the most wonderful designs, if you can't get them made or sold, then you might as well not be in the business." Born in Dublin, he studied fashion at the Grafton Academy of Dress

LEFT **After graduating from Dublin's Grafton Academy of Dress Design in 1987, Cuan Hanly spent seven years working for England's most successful menswear designer, Paul Smith. During this period he never produced any clothes of his own, but as these two stylish suits from his spring/summer 1998 range show, he learnt a great deal about simple good design from his time with Smith.**

Men are notoriously more conservative dressers than women, and men's designers have to venture carefully when it comes to new ideas. Cuan Hanly understands this situation very well, as this shirt from his spring/summer 1998 collection shows. Plainness is relieved only by the broad bands of contrasting colour used on the hem and ends of the sleeves.

Design and after his graduation in 1987, he moved to London. There he went to work with England's leading menswear designer, Paul Smith. But Cuan Hanly's years in England were spent honing his retail rather than his design skills. He began on the shopfloor of Paul Smith's Covent Garden outlet and gradually moved up through stock-control to become the group's retail co-ordinator. "The lessons I learnt with Paul were to do with business rather than design," he says. But by 1994, "I'd sort of progressed through the company and I wanted to come back to Ireland." He took a position with John Rocha where, once more, his expertise outside the field of design was put to use as he assumed responsibility for sales and marketing in Europe and the Far East.

Eventually, however, Cuan Hanly's initial training as a fashion designer demanded expression and in 1996 he was able to win backing from A Wear to produce a relatively inexpensive range of menswear, which he did for the following two years. "His brief was to be contemporary but commercial," said A Wear's then chief executive, Deirdre Kelly, "and as far as I'm concerned, he has achieved both." Inevitably, the discreet influence of Paul Smith may be seen in his work which shows a strong belief in the primacy of good tailoring. "Having worked with Paul for so long, of course I have the same attitude," he concurred at the time his first collection appeared. "I think I've the same no-nonsense approach." Like those of Smith, Cuan

Hanly's clothes achieve effect by simple means such as different shades of the same colour used in the bands of a shirt, or a jacket cut a little more sharply than usual. He likes to work with well-established suiting fabrics such as moleskin and wool crepe pinstripe, but will use technologically advanced materials too provided they serve his purpose. "Obviously, compared to women's clothes menswear doesn't change rapidly from season to season. Instead, there tends to be a lot more innovation in the fabric that's used and the finish on it. So with my collections, I'm trying to keep them classic but contemporary and moving forward." Cuan Hanly has put his retail experience to good use and opened a shop in Dublin's Temple Bar District. He argues that young design graduates need to be encouraged to take risks and given support to start their own businesses.

Lucy Downes

One designer who chose not to wait for assistance but just set up a company herself is Lucy Downes. Like Cuan Hanly, she is keenly aware of commercial realities, in her case thanks to a degree in economics and business taken before she went on to study fashion at the National College of Art and Design. While still a student, Lucy Downes was offered a job with Donna Karan's DKNY label, having worked with the company during summer holidays in New York. From the start, she showed a keen interest in knitwear, winning a post-graduate award from the Irish Knitwear Exporters' Guild, but at DKNY she was employed in the footwear division from 1994 to 1998. Now she says this digression into another section of fashion was advantageous, not least because it avoided early pigeon-holing. "The DKNY experience was really beneficial," she told the *Sunday Business Post* in September 1999. "It let me see how other people approach business issues." However, after four years in New York, she chose to return to her native Dublin and start her own label, specialising once more in knits.

Her company, called Sphere One, produced its first collection in autumn 1999 and offered luxurious cashmere knits in a variety of colours from sombre charcoal grey to brilliant fuchsia pink. This range combined tradition – the Irish history of working with knits – with modernity. Cashmere was used in an innovative form; all the

Could any designer working in Ireland ignore the country's strong tradition of knitwear? Our inclement climate certainly encourages its manufacture, as does the rich variety of patterns. Here Cuan Hanly offers a sweater for men in which the surface design has been restricted to one band of raised diamonds across the chest, paying homage to the Aran knit without being in thrall to it.

designs were knitted in single ply and in extremely large shapes which were then felted down to the correct size by a boiling technique that even her manufacturers found difficult to master successfully. Furthermore, the finished garments were not the customary cashmere twinsets but unusual items such as halternecks, held in place by solid silver chokers, and hooded tops with drawstrings. The inspiration here was clearly 1990s sportswear and its ability to be dressed up or down according to circumstances.

In this respect, Lucy Downes's sensibility has clearly been influenced by her time spent in America. She talks about the "notion of versatility in clothes" and suggests that "the modern sophisticated person is interested in having a simple wardrobe of modern designs in luxury fabrics and getting rid of lots of other stuff." In her first season, she found three outlets in Dublin keen to carry her clothes and this number looks set to expand over the coming year. Identifying and then targeting a market has become essential for designers who wish to thrive in the fashion industry at the end of the twentieth century. Just as almost fifty years earlier Sybil Connolly had made a point of identifying and wooing potential clients, so Lucy Downes remarks, "There's a small critical mass of young people with taste and money and an eye for something a bit different. I knew the market was there; it was just a question of fine-tuning the prices to suit them."

That Marc O'Neill, Cuan Hanly and Lucy Downes share certain characteristics in their approach to fashion suggests they represent a new breed of Irish designer. All of them are simultaneously sensible and ambitious, tracking the course of their careers with care. They also have in common a pleasure in resolving technical challenges and in overcoming the problems of production. They understand the importance of knowing the market's demands and responding to these without sacrificing creative flair. Finally, that creativity is European rather than Irish in spirit. While the three designers are all happy to be based in their own country, they recognise their work must be as attractive to the overseas as the domestic customer. In the new millennium and in fashion, there is no place for nationalistic insularity.

From her very first collection, one of
Lucy Downes's best-selling pieces was
the simple scarf shown here. Made from
cashmere, it came with a little loop in
mohair and was inexpensive enough to
appeal to a young market.

into the new millennium

At the start of a new millennium, Irish fashion is stronger than at any time in its past. It is also better appreciated internationally and more widely exported than ever before. Fifty years ago, when fashion in Ireland first began to emerge, it seemed weak and vulnerable compared to the comparatively strong indigenous clothing industry. Those positions have now been reversed; the Irish clothing sector barely exists any longer, but Ireland produces a large number of fashion designers who choose to establish their own businesses. They enjoy advantages unknown to their predecessors, the most important being a healthy domestic economy in which the culture of success is encouraged.

Looking back over the last half-century, Irish fashion emerged wonderfully and unexpectedly around 1950 thanks to the efforts of a small group of designers, predominantly women. With great rapidity, it established an international reputation and during the 1960s sustained this through the growth of exports to Britain and the United States. But the recession of the 1970s, combined with the decline of both couture and the demand for traditional Irish fabrics, made this decade particularly tough for the country's fashion industry. After 1980, there appeared a new group of designers whose sensibility was more international than their predecessors and whose Irish clientele demanded a greater awareness of contemporary global trends. Many of those same designers continued to enjoy success during the 1990s when their number was augmented, at home and abroad, by younger names whose presence ensured that, by the end of the century, Irish fashion had a higher profile than at any time since the 1950s.

But the industry's current good fortune ought not to be exaggerated. In global terms, Ireland remains a minor player. It is dependent on a handful of names and shows little evidence of an ability to capitalise on whatever attention fashion in Ireland does receive. Many observers in this field comment on fashion's failure to make the most of the global goodwill engendered by some of the country's other creative industries. Irish writers have always been greatly admired, but in the 1990s the success experienced in such areas such as pop music and film meant that Ireland developed a worldwide reputation as a centre of contemporary cultural excellence. During the same decade, the tourist industry blossomed as Ireland became a fashionable holiday destination. In the first half of 1999, for example, the number of people travelling to the country was ten per cent higher than it had been just a year earlier. Dublin, for many years shunned by tourists in preference for more rural parts of the country, was now seen internationally as a stylish capital; in 1994, British *Elle* proclaimed the city to be the hippest place on the planet.

Goodwill, of course, is not a tangible quality which can be measured. Nonetheless, its benefits are real and so too is the feeling that Irish fashion has yet to make the most of the opportunities now available. "Ireland culturally has been much more on the map in the last ten years, certainly in terms of film and rock music," says Godfrey Deeny. "I don't think we've exploited our strengths in fashion to anything like the same extent. We haven't taken full advantage of our fabrics, our imagery, the sense of naturalness and beauty. There's been a major failure of the industry there."

One fundamental change which has occurred over the past half century is that fashion has become a global industry in which neither design nor manufacturing is exclusive to any one country. Ireland, of course, has always recognised the importance of the international market since its domestic business alone has never been substantial enough. From the very beginning, exports played an important part. So too, today, does tapping into the world fashion circuit. Whereas journalists and buyers in the 1950s were willing to visit Dublin in order to see the latest collection from Sybil Connolly, her successors cannot hope for the same treatment. "Fashion is now based around four major cities – Paris, London, New York and Milan," John Rocha explains. "The buyers and press only give a certain amount of time of the year to certain places and so it would be impossible for me to say, I'm going to show here in Dublin. The ideal is for designers to pick the place they feel most comfortable with and show there. I've picked London."

Given that Irish designers who want to maintain a successful business have to depend on exports and on staging shows overseas, can the fashion industry here still have its own distinct identity or will it be subsumed into a global mass culture? The traditional image of Ireland as a country unspoilt and almost untouched by modernity is a very powerful one and has been heavily exploited for much of the twentieth century. As Andrew

Tucker remarks, "Before I became involved with Irish fashion, I'd this kind of pastoral image of the country which I think is one a lot of people have. You look at the tourist brochures and always see a dry stone wall and some ponies; it's terribly predictable and doesn't reflect what's coming out of Ireland at the moment."

That traditional view of Ireland enjoys enormous popularity in many countries. In France, for example, Enterprise Ireland's Jim Maguire can point to the success of the Irish shops stocking Aran sweaters, tweed caps and similar items. There are now some sixty-five such outlets in France, including the locally-owned Le Comptoir Irlandais chain, and since they have an annual turnover in the region of £20 million there is obviously a vested interest in supporting Ireland's traditional image and industries. According to Jim Maguire, "that image is used by quite a few Irish manufacturers and it's both positive and negative. It launches them into a particular market niche which is quite small but does exist. However, it can mean that they are precluded from mainstream markets because the traditional look is hard to match up with any other clothing."

Here lies the fundamental conundrum for Irish fashion. The industry is fortunate to possess a very strong traditional identity but exploiting this means risking isolation in the fashion market. Furthermore, just as dry stone walls and white-washed cottages do not reflect the reality of Ireland in the new millennium, nor do Aran sweaters and tweed jackets provide an accurate view of Irish fashion today. "I do think Ireland has a very strong brand image," Cuan Hanly confirms, "but I'm not sure it's the traditional one of the Aran sweater and cloth cap – it has moved on from that. I don't mean to say this is because Dublin is the country's capital, but I think the city has developed fairly rapidly and it is now seen as the brand image of Ireland, not the Aran sweater."

Certainly, a traditional garment like the Aran no longer reflects the state of Irish fashion in which diversity is the most striking characteristic. Many designers such as Marc O'Neill or Louise Kennedy produce work of an international sensibility; its Irish origins are barely discernible. This is a worldwide phenomenon. As designer Michael Mortell points out, "If you bought a copy of French *Vogue* in 1963 or 1964, from the front cover to the back every designer would look the same and so were the advertisements. Whereas if you buy a fashion magazine now, every page has a different look. There isn't a common thread and that's as true of Ireland as anywhere else."

However, some of the country's designers, for example Lainey Keogh, manage to be both Irish and global in their designs. What she has in common with her peers in Ireland is a uniqueness of vision, a sense that she is one of a kind. "The big Irish stars are all very individualistic and trying to find some common ground between them maybe isn't such a good idea," Paula Reed comments. "We're all Europeans now, so pursuing nationalism in design as an end in itself isn't such a good idea." It is interesting that designers whose identity is very powerfully Irish tend to perform best in the home market; the examples of Mary Gregory and Ciaran Sweeney, two labels known for their surface embellishment of clothing, spring to mind here. It would seem that in order to develop a strong export market, the amount of ethnicity must be moderated.

At the same time, the end of the twentieth century saw a revived interest in hand-craft and distinctive differences in fashion. Many commentators of the industry have noted how globalism encourages uniformity and this inevitably causes a reaction in favour of the individual. Ireland's history of handwork in areas such as weaving and knitting obviously stands to her advantage here. "One of the things Irish fashion has brought to the European stage of fashion is this gorgeous appreciation of craft," confirms Paula Reed. "We've always had that but maybe in the past it looked a bit hokey. People like John Rocha have taken those fantastic details, married them with technology and made them into something which looks very modern but very particular to their background, history and culture." Cuan Hanly's description of his own work as classic but contemporary seems to suggest a way forward for the entire Irish fashion industry. The ideal, it seems, is to produce work which has some but not too much ethnic identity, expressed less through the use of traditional forms or motifs than through the employment of historical skills which have been lost elsewhere. The survival of these skills, perhaps more than anything else, is what sets Irish fashion apart from its equivalents elsewhere in Europe.

The question remains, however, whether a small country can hope to develop a strong fashion industry in the global market.

Obviously, as a manufacturing base, Ireland cannot compete any longer with North Africa and the Far East. But the design business may thrive even when clothes must be made elsewhere. The most frequently cited instance of what can be achieved is the history of Belgian fashion in the 1990s. Twenty years ago, Belgium – like Ireland – was universally regarded as a fashion peripheral, a player so minor that the country was believed to have produced no designers of any note. Within a decade, a large number of Belgian designers such as Dries Van Noten, Martin Margiela, Ann Demeulemeester and Dirk Bikkembergs had become important participants in the global fashion market.

The success of the Belgians offers a number of useful lessons to Irish fashion. It is noteworthy, for example, that these designers, while original in their work, did not try to alter the industry in which they operate; they show their collections in Paris during its twice-yearly fashion week, and in all other aspects of production and distribution conform to the dictates of the business. Belgium now has a body of great designers but does not attempt to keep them to herself; nor should Ireland try to do so. "Size isn't really an impediment," says Godfrey Deeny, "nor is the lack of a big local market. What you have to do is think in a very international way. You have to invest money and show in the fashion capitals and you've got to keep yourself very open to global trends. Any industry, and especially fashion, depends on a number of stars who can lead the way. We still need another few, we need half a dozen more designers who could make up a real school rather than a number of people who are seen as exceptional."

The puzzle remains how Belgium, or any other country, should be able to produce the requisite number of fashion stars. Certain states such as France and Italy have the advantage of a long history in the field. Michael Mortell points out that Ireland's ready-to-wear industry developed in the late 1970s at the same time as that in Italy. "Before people like Armani and Versace came along in Milan, you really only had couturiers in Rome. The difference was that the Italians had this big machine, the native textile industry, and it supported the designers while they supported it. There was a happy marriage that we didn't have around us." Without sufficiently strong support from other related areas of the business and from government (again something which is commonplace in France and

Italy, where fashion is recognised as an important export industry), designers are always going to feel isolated. Lainey Keogh is particularly outspoken on this subject. "I find it perfectly impossible to run an international business based in Ireland," she says. "I'm frustrated with the limitations of being based in this country. There's no infrastructure. I don't source anything here, no yarn, nothing. We create all our own accessories by hand, there are no resources other than the ones we produce ourselves. For me, being in Ireland has been a very romantic, heartfelt thing but I cannot continue to do what I see as the way forward in the way I've been doing it here. It's impossible."

Lainey Keogh argues that fashion needs nurturing and that this process must start in colleges if young talent is to be encouraged. That is a point constantly reiterated by many designers, who point out the successful Belgians all emerged from one institution, Antwerp's Royal Academy of Arts. "I think a lot of the success of Irish fashion will come from its colleges," Sharon Wauchob argues. "That's one way Irish fashion can really become a force to be reckoned with. I saw this when I was at St Martin's College where it was not just the teaching but the interaction among diverse people who were there and had a desire to achieve that made the difference. That's also what happened in Belgium; because of the competition between the designers, they created something new. And then they started to compete on the international circuit."

Encouragement of young talent is clearly crucial and this has never been more possible. Ireland's economy is now sufficiently strong for designers to run their own businesses from the country, provided they recognise the importance of overseas markets. At the end of the 1990s, Irish fashion was already making a global impact out of proportion with its actual size; tellingly, in 1999 clothing accounted for just one per cent of Ireland's total export figure of £31 billion. But the industry will need additional support. John Rocha, for example, argues that more investment in new technology for the textile industry is needed and he, like other designers, remarks that many of the country's manufacturers have not kept up with advances in fabric production. Equally, and perhaps paradoxically, hand-craft workers need to be nurtured. Lainey Keogh laments the loss of domestic talent which has withered away through neglect. "I'd wonder why every exquisite weaving mill in the west of Ireland was not supported by the State or anybody else," she observes. "The wonderful yarn spinning available in pockets of Ireland was healthy and well in the fifties and sixties but this was not nurtured. I feel the industry went for the money and not for creation. It wasn't balanced."

And yet, it could be that the combination of traditional craft with new technology might distinguish Irish fashion from that designed elsewhere and make it competitive on the world market. Given sufficient support, therefore, the industry in Ireland can only grow stronger. It is, after all, a young industry and still learning its own strengths and weaknesses. Fifty years after first emerging, Irish fashion certainly has the potential to enjoy a prosperous future.

The Author, Daniel Productions Ltd and the Publishers are grateful to the following for permission to use their photographs/illustrations, given for use in this book for the most part by the designers as follows:

Illustrations for:

Cleo - Mike Bunn.

Sybil Connolly - Richard Dormer

Paul Costello - David Bailey; Chris Moore.

Pat Crowley - Neil Campbell Sharp; Tony Higgins.

Lucy Downes - Nick West.

Irene Gilbert - Trevor Hart; Irene Gilbert\

Cuan Hanly - Barry McCall; Murrish Mournaghan.

Patrick Howard - Neil Campbell Sharp.

Inis Meain - Fintan Friel.

Michael Jacobs - Neil Campbell Sharp.

Ib Jorgensen - Tony Higgins; Ursula Steiger; International Woollen Secretariat.

Jen Kelly - Barry McCall.

Louise Kennedy - Ian Bradshaw; Tony Higgins; Barry McCall.

Lainey Keogh - Tony Higgins; Conor Horgan; Kay Keogh; Chris Moore; Amelia Stein.

Daryl Kerrigan - Dan Lecca.

Lyn-Mar - Shane McCarthy; Pat McHugh.

Richard Lewis - Roy Esmonde; Breffini Ryan; Ursula Steiger.

Michael Mortell - Mike Bunn; Tony Higgins.

Neilli Mulcahy - Bobby Dawson; Tony Higgins.

Lorcan Mullany - Natasha Bult; Express Newspapers; Lorcan Mullany.

Peter O'Brien - Pascal Therme.

Mary O'Donnell - Tony Higgins; Sean O'Sullivan; Ursula Steiger.

Marc O'Neil - Conor Horgan; Barry McCall; Eamonn McLoughlin.

Quin & Donnelly - Brendan Bourke; Tony Higgins; Barry McCall; Ursula Steiger.

Jacqueline Quinn - Tara O'Reilly.

John Rocha - Mike Bunn; Niall McInerney.

Michelina Stacpoole - Tony Higgins; Ursula Steiger.

Philip Treacy - Chris Heads; Robert Fairer.

Sharon Wauchob - Joshua Neville.

Thomas Wolfangel - Neil Campbell Sharp.